LOYAL TO KING BILLY

ROBERT G. CRAWFORD

Loyal to King Billy

A Portrait of the Ulster Protestants

C. HURST & COMPANY, LONDON
ST. MARTIN'S PRESS, NEW YORK

First published in the United Kingdom by
C. Hurst & Co. (Publishers) Ltd., London
and in the United States of America by
St. Martin's Press, Inc.,
175 Fifth Avenue, New York, NY 10010.
All rights reserved.
© Robert G. Crawford, 1987
Printed in England on long-life paper

ISBNs
Hurst cased   : 1-85065-029-2
Hurst paper   : 1-85065-030-6
(*St Martin's*) : 0-312-01304-3

Library of Congress Cataloging-in-Publication Data
Crawford, Robert G. (Robert George), 1927-
  Loyal to King Billy.

  Bibliography: p.
  1. Ulster (Northern Ireland and Ireland)—History.
2. Ulster (Northern Ireland and Ireland)—Politics
and government. 3. Protestants—Ulster (Northern
Ireland and Ireland)—History. I. Title.
DA990.U46C73   1987   941.6082'08823   87-20541
ISBN 0-312-01304-3

*To my Mother and Father
in grateful remembrance*

FOREWORD

People ask in despair, and with growing impatience, whether there can ever be a solution to the 'Ulster problem', which seems to get steadily more intractable, with the piling up of hatred and lust for revenge at each new outrage. Ever more horrific crimes seem to indicate a draining away of common humanity, and the voices of reason and compassion fall on deaf ears. In just this despair, the feeling that the only solution is total victory for one side and total annihilation for the other may be spreading beyond the small groups of extremists who stop at nothing. But the very history and geography of Ireland make such a solution impossible — even if the human spirit that is still true to its name did not reject it completely. The impetus behind the ill-fated and possibly ill-planned Peace Movement of the 1970s must have been the right one. There must be some way of bringing the extremists to their senses other than the total exhaustion and total destruction of war.

Can yet another book about Ulster do any good? Before saying what this book is, or seeks to be, perhaps I should say what it is not. It is not designed to compete with specialised and scholarly works on Northern Ireland, many of which I have consulted in the course of writing it. It does not pretend to be based on primary, unpublished sources, and thus to present new facts or original research. And it does not embody any attempt to present the Ulster Protestant 'case', as that concept is generally understood — a case which, by its nature, must be blind to the interests of other parties, most notably the Ulster Catholics.

It *does* draw on my own birth and upbringing as an Ulster Protestant; on my ministry in the Presbyterian Church of Ireland, in Ulster; and on my years of ministry and teaching outside Ulster. Does the last of these — which has removed me from the turmoil, tragedy, fear and passion which might well have engulfed the lives of myself and my family had we remained in Ulster — act as a disqualification? The Ulster Protestants whom I describe by the adjective 'extreme' would probably say that it does — that an expatriate Ulsterman has ceased not only to feel as they do, but really to understand any longer what motivates their words and actions.

I naturally run the risk of having my credentials dismissed on these grounds, but it has to be asked too: would an Ulster Protestant living in Ulster be able to consider objectively his people's religious and political culture, and see its faults as well as its undoubted virtues? My purpose, while in no way wedded to a particular political viewpoint, is to enlarge a little the understanding of Ulster Protestants in the world outside Ulster. Due to the antics of an unrepresentative few, they are far down the road to losing irrevocably the battle for the world's hearts and minds —, by comparison with their declared enemies, who certainly do not deserve the more sympathetic image they seem to enjoy in the eyes of many sophisticated, liberal, right-thinking people. As an Ulsterman I find this distressing. I do not ask the world to love my people. I do ask for intelligent understanding.

Finally, I wish to acknowledge my debt to two people who gave me invaluable help in the preparation of the book: my publisher, Mr Christopher Hurst, and Miss Nomfuneko Phoebe Ndemka, who typed the manuscript with skill and speed.

Autumn 1987 R.G.C.

CONTENTS

Foreword   *page* vii
Checklist of Parties and Paramilitary Organisations   x
Map of Northern Ireland   xii

CHAPTERS

1. Living in Ulster   1
2. The Historical Factor   19
3. The Religious Factor   40
4. The Rise and Fall of Stormont   61
5. Direct Rule   85
6. A Comparison: the Afrikaner   106
7. The Way Forward   118

APPENDIXES

A. Documents on Ulster's History: Extracts and Commentary   130
B. The *Westminster Confession of Faith*, 1643: Extracts and Commentary   143

Index   148

CHECKLIST OF PARTIES AND PARAMILITARY ORGANISATIONS

Alliance Party. A Catholic and Protestant party founded on 21 April 1970 under the leadership of a Belfast solicitor, Oliver John Napier.

Apprentice Boys. A Protestant body which annually celebrates its namesakes who in 1688 shut the gates of Londonderry against James II. It has links with the Orange Order. The celebration on 12 August each year often creates violence and riots.

'B Specials'. An auxiliary force of the Royal Ulster Constabulary. Founded in 1920 to help defend Ulster, they were Protestant and came to be hated by the Catholics. They were disbanded by the British Government in 1969, amid much protest from hardline Unionists, and replaced by the Ulster Defence Regiment.

Civil Rights Association. Founded in 1967, it drew the world's attention, with its marches and protests, to the discrimination practised by the Stormont regime against Catholics. It gradually became associated with the I.R.A.

Democratic Unionist Party. Founded in 1972 and led by the Reverend Ian Paisley, it has a strong working-class membership, many of whom also belong to Paisley's Free Presbyterian Church. It is militant and right-wing.

Irish Republican Army. The traditional foe of the English, its activity culminating in the fight for Irish independence (1919–21). In the post-1969 campaign in Ulster it split into the Provisional I.R.A. (favours war to win) and the Official I.R.A. (favours political and social action).

Irish National Liberation Army. A guerrilla group, responsible for the assassination at Westminster of Airey Neave, a senior British Conservative Member of Parliament, in 1979. It split from the Official I.R.A., and contended for a continued campaign of violence.

Irish Republican Socialist Party. The political wing of the Irish National Liberation Army. Left-wing and nationalistic.

People's Democracy. Founded by students in 1968, it quickly showed left-wing tendencies and militancy. Its influence has waned over the years.

Republican Clubs. The political wing of the Official I.R.A. It holds a number of elected seats in local Councils.

Royal Ulster Constabulary. Founded in 1922 it had about 10 per cent Catholic membership. It was reformed in 1969 and, despite much criticism, remains the security force for the Province.

Sinn Fein ('Ourselves Alone'). Political party founded in 1905 by Arthur Griffith. It held that the Union with England was illegal, and that Ireland should have its own government. It has always represented the core of the Republican tradition. There is an ill-defined connection with the I.R.A.

Social Democratic and Labour Party. Founded in 1970 by nationalists and republicans. It has presented a good image to the media, and gained much sympathy for the Catholic cause. Its leaders — Gerry Fitt (now Lord Fitt), 1970–80, and John Hume since 1980 — have been highly respected.

Ulster Defence Association. Founded in 1969, it is a Protestant defence force which has remained legal, although its members have been convicted of murders. It attempted to negotiate peace terms with the I.R.A. and others in 1977, but the initiative only lasted a short time.

Ulster Defence Regiment. A unit of the British Army, formed in 1970 to replace the 'B' Specials, with part-time and full-time members. There is a small Catholic membership.

Ulster Protestant Volunteers. Founded in 1965 by the Revd Ian Paisley, it is a paramilitary body which caused violence during the premiership of Captain Terence O'Neill. It came to an end about 1969.

Ulster Unionist Party. Right-wing and capitalist, with strong links to the United Kingdom's Conservative Party, it was the dominant party from the beginnings of Stormont. After various splits in the 1970s, it became known as the Official Unionist Party.

Ulster Volunteer Force. Formed about 1965, it took the name of an earlier body set up in 1912 to oppose Home Rule. Made illegal after a number of murders in 1966, it went underground and continued sectarian killings. It is still active.

Ulster Workers' Council. Powerful body of Ulster Protestant trade unionists which opposed the power-sharing executive of Brian Faulkner and Gerry Fitt in 1974. It closed down the power stations and helped to topple the power-sharing government.

Unionist Party of Northern Ireland. One of the splits from the Ulster Unionist Party, created by Brian Faulkner to follow a more moderate line.

United Ulster Unionist Council. An alliance of the Official Unionist Party, the Democratic Unionist Party, and the Vanguard Unionist Party formed to fight the United Kingdom general election of 1974 and the election for the 1975 Convention. It was unable to preserve unity, and is no longer active.

United Ulster Unionist Movement. Originally part of William Craig's Vanguard Unionist Party, but split away when Craig became reconciled with the official Unionist Party. The leader is Ernest Baird.

Vanguard Unionist Party. Established in 1973 by William Craig, who had founded the Ulster Vanguard a year earlier, as a break-away from the Unionist Party, then led by Brian Faulkner. It favoured the total independence of Ulster. Not active after c. 1976.

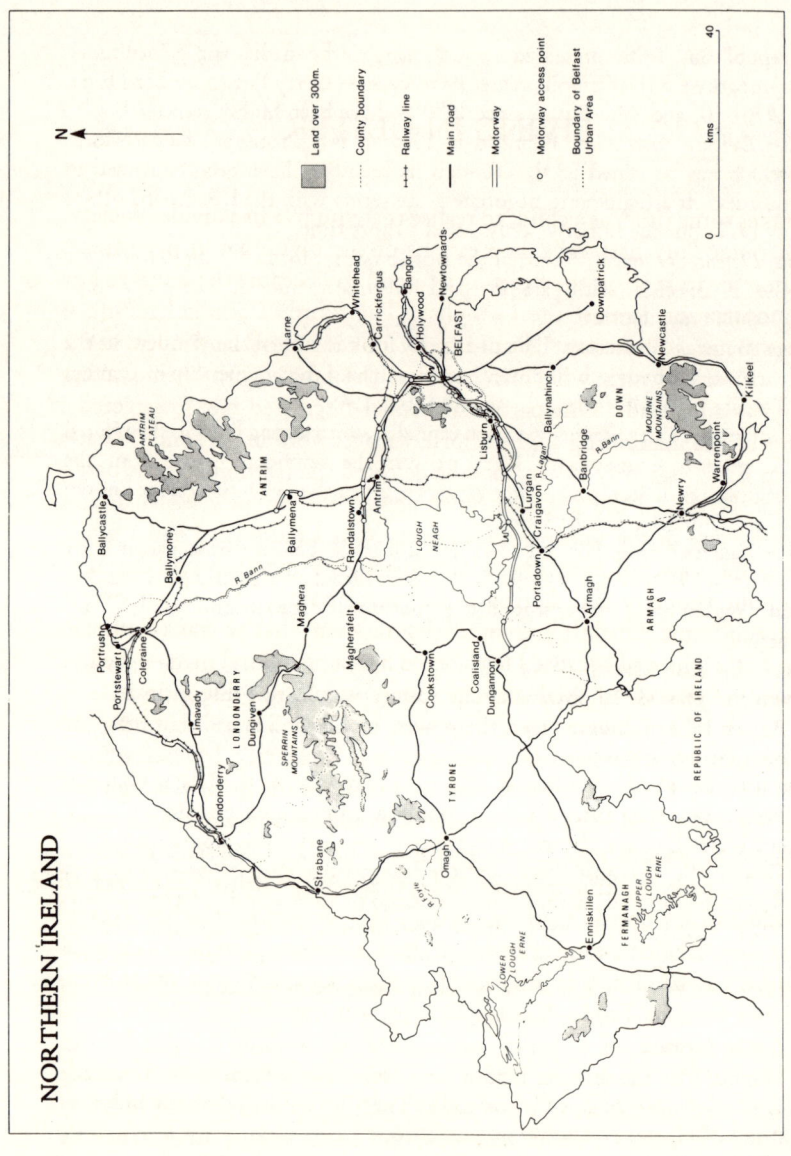

Reproduced, with permission, from Paul A. Compton, *Northern Ireland: A Census Atlas*, Dublin: Gill and Macmillan, 1978.

1
LIVING IN ULSTER

It takes some time, as a child, to realise that you live in a divided society. But one of my first vivid impressions of the division was my parents telling me to keep off the street on a certain day because there was to be a demonstration against the Catholics. The word 'Catholic' meant as little to me as 'Protestant', but I eagerly looked out of the window at the line of serious men who marched past the house with their waving banners and bands. One particular banner fascinated me: it depicted a long-haired man riding a white horse with a sword in his hand. 'That's King Billy,' said my father, 'and he defeated the Catholics at the battle of the Boyne.' I did not care much about 'the Boyne', which I later learned was in the south of the country, but I did wish I had a white horse and a sword! Later I heard that those same marchers had damaged Catholic property and destroyed the petrol pumps of a garage owner near our home. I hadn't known till that moment that he was a Catholic, but I was annoyed because I considered him a nice, kind man — he had given me sweets. I hoped that the supply would not discontinue.

At school I discovered that there were no Catholics and that they had their own schools where they were educated separately. My best subject was history. I loved hearing about the exploits of the British, which was the main diet, and hoped that one day I would see and work with members of the great British commonwealth of nations. The sense of adventure, fair play, fighting qualities and courage of the British, as portrayed in our history books, made me proud, for our history teacher stressed that we were British and not Irish. Indeed, the story of Ireland's struggle against the English was only mentioned incidentally, and when eventually I went to Trinity College Dublin, southern friends were amazed at my ignorance.

We lived by the sea near Belfast but often travelled north to the seaside resorts of Portrush and Portstewart. Usually we stopped for lunch at Ballymena, which is about half-way, and I was immediately struck by the speech of the people. 'They are Scots', said mother, 'and you must not play with them at Portrush because you will pick up their accent!' I liked the accent myself and secretly vowed to imitate it, but was attracted by Dad's story. A stranger, he said, was travelling towards Ballymena and was not sure that he was on the right road. So he asked a farmer: 'Is this the main road to Ballymena?' 'It is,' he replied and the further you go the meaner [pronounced 'mainer'] they get!' He laughed heartily at the pun, and in order to make sure that I understood, added: 'The Scots love the crown but they love the half-crown better!'

My father did not belong to the Orange Order and had no desire to join it, but he never missed the great Twelfth of July parade. On that day he put on his Sunday suit, and best bowler hat, and his shoes had to be brightly polished. Then, having inspected that I was well attired, he took me into the centre of Belfast to see the Orangemen. He explained that Orange was the colour of the Dutch flag, and King Billy had come from Holland. The city was a mass of colour with arches and bunting of every description but the red, white and blue predominated. The men wore orange sashes, carried huge banners, and followed different bands. They came not only from all over the country but from all over world. The crowds applauded and women danced in the streets. The big Lambeg drum was fascinating as huge muscular men using light canes beat it with rhythmic strokes while the perspiration poured down their cheeks. Later in life I saw Nigerians beating their drums with the same wild abandonment, and remembered the scene.

The music was varied, but one tune was repeated which stirred the blood of the men and caused the women to dance, '*The Sash*':

> *It is old but it is beautiful,*
> *Its colours they are fine.*
> *It was worn at Derry, Aughrim,*
> *Enniskillen and the Boyne.*
> *My father wore it when a youth*
> *In bygone days of yore;*
> *On the Twelfth I proudly wear*
> *The Sash my father wore.*

I didn't understand then, but learned later, that the places mentioned in '*The Sash*' were where battles had been fought, and celebrated the defeat of the Catholics.

I wondered why my Dad did not walk in this parade with a stick and white gloves, but when I asked him he just shook his head and murmured something about 'bigotry'. There are many stories told about this parade but I think of two in particular. An Englishman, viewing the spectacle with delight and some bewilderment, turns to a loyal son of Ulster and asks: 'I say, old chap, could you tell me what this means?' The 'native' stared at him and muttered 'The Twelfth'. 'I know', persisted the Englishman, 'but what does "Twelfth" mean?' 'Man, are you ignorant,' answered the Ulsterman, 'away home and read your Bible!' The second story is about a small boy who jumped and clapped his hands with delight as the marchers passed by, and said to his mother: 'When I grow up, could I put on the Sash and march in this parade?' She looked at him sadly and replied: 'You will never march in that parade, PATRICK!'

Sometimes we followed the Orangemen to the field at Finaghy (a suburb of Belfast) through streets that had the walls of the houses newly daubed in huge lettering: 'No Pope here', 'Down with the I.R.A.', 'Up the Orange Order', 'Fenians out', 'No surrender', 'Remember 1690', 'Burn the Pope'. I said to my father that they did not seem to like this man called Pope, but he only smiled. In the field where the Orangemen congregated, ministers of religion and other speakers seemed to get quite excited about the battle of the Boyne and what it meant today. There was much applause and shouts of 'Hear, Hear', 'Down with De Valera' and 'No surrender'. I was more interested in the ice cream and the lemonade.

When I was twelve or thirteen, I met the fireside philosopher, a bachelor who worked in the shipyard and lived in our village. My aunt owned a shop and he would come after work to buy groceries and talk. My brother and I sitting in the living room would hear him going on and on, while my aunt patiently listened — he was her best customer. Eventually she could endure standing at the counter no longer and was forced to invite him into the living room. He would protest for another fifteen minutes, but eventually he always came. We regaled him with questions about everything, but his main interest was politics. Invariably he talked about the British and their exploits and somehow always managed to mention his hero, Winston Churchill. When we dared to contradict he would retort: 'That's a terminological inexactitude', and pause to see the effect. 'I thought you wouldn't understand the meaning of that,' he would say triumphantly, 'it was a favourite phrase of Churchill's. If your education had not been so sadly neglected you would have known it.' We would laugh while our aunt vainly strove to signal to us that we must not encourage him to stay. He was dogmatic, had little knowledge, and had ceased to learn. He wasn't religious and did not talk much about the Orange Order, but he was certain that the Catholics were doing all they could to get us into a United Ireland. His strong, harsh voice and the dogmatism with which he spoke still haunt me. I have often wondered if he really did not know that Winston Churchill, unlike his father Lord Randolph, favoured Home

Rule for Ireland and that his car would have been overturned in Belfast if the mob had not seen that his wife was with him and stopped.

In my early teens I attended a commercial school to prepare for entry into business and studied accounting with typing and shorthand. There I met a Catholic girl — I didn't know at first that she was Catholic because she had a Protestant name, being the daughter of what the locals called 'a mixed marriage'. The Catholic Church insists that the children of such a marriage must be brought up as Catholics. She talked little about her Protestant father whom she appeared not to admire very much, but much more of her mother and what she had learned from her. We used to walk home together and spent hours talking until my mother heard about it and the liaison was immediately forbidden. This did not upset me too much because when the girl had told me that she was a Catholic I was greatly shocked. The memory of my first glimpse of the local Catholic church with its candles, images, Stations of the Cross and smell of incense had so frightened me as a child that I could not imagine being part of it. It was such a contrast to the modern Presbyterian church that I attended.

Another contact with Catholics developed at home. There was just one Catholic family in our middle-class suburb, and I liked them a lot better than some of the Protestants we knew. I used to play games with two of the boys, and a Protestant boy joined us. He had the reputation of being a great fighter and quite often our games were interrupted by his pugnacious instincts or by other boys coming to challenge him to a boxing contest. One day in playing tricks upon us he pushed one of the Catholic boys into a river and ruined his clothes. When I remonstrated with him about this he replied, 'Stop complaining, he's only a Catholic.' Such an assumption of superiority, I felt, was completely unjustified since the Catholics were so much better than him both in manners and general behaviour.

My mother was Anglican (Church of Ireland) and my father a Presbyterian. He was not much interested in churchgoing and had to be forced by my mother to go. She eventually got tired of this and took me to the local Church of Ireland where her former rector from the country now officiated. He was a kindly man but I hated all the kneeling, and the prayers seemed so repetitive that I lost interest. However, the local Presbyterian Church had a famous Boys' Brigade with over 100 members so I joined it. The Brigade met nearly every night for drill, gymnastics or band practice (they had both bugles and bagpipes) and I became a side drummer and centre-forward in the football team. We had to attend church but the sermons were long and boring and we usually sat at the back and chatted, to the disgust of the elders. The captain of the Brigade was an Ulster Protestant of distinction. He told us 'yarns' at Bible class of the exploits of missionaries, adventurers, preachers and so on, and we sang the 'B.B.' hymns with great gusto. He had devoted his life to the Brigade and displayed an impressive friendliness to each boy individually. When he died the entire local community turned out for the funeral.

We never played football against any Catholic teams, but I used to go and watch Celtic (Catholic) and Linfield. These two teams reflected their counterparts in Scotland, and the blue of Rangers was worn by Linfield. One Saturday I was watching a very skilful Celtic team and applauded vigorously when they made a clever move. Suddenly I noticed with apprehension that there was a silence around me. Then somebody nudged me and shouted, 'You know where you should be — over there', pointing to a mass of people on the other side of the stadium. They were the Catholics, and the Protestants that I was among didn't like my applause for Celtic. After the game, which Celtic won, the Protestants rushed across the pitch shouting and hurling things at the Catholics. The police intervened but eventually these encounters between the two teams came to an end after a series of ugly incidents, and Celtic decided to leave the league. But my greatest experience of football was watching England play Northern Ireland at Windsor Park, Belfast. Before the match I was granted an interview with Peter Doherty, the idol of Irish fans, so that I could write something for the B.B. magazine. He was one of the most impressive Catholics I have ever met, so informal and friendly. As he shaved, he chatted about football, and explained some of the techniques which had made him and Carter two of the best inside-forwards in the English league. England that day had probably their best-ever forward line: Matthews, Carter, Lawton, Mortenson, Finney. The gigantic Swift was in goal and Matthews excelled. England won eight goals to four, but the Irish goals were scored by Peter Doherty.

In my first job I met 'Paddy'. He was the only Catholic in the office and enjoyed jokes, but not those made about his religion and his politics. His prejudice showed itself at lunchtime in the bar where he often broke into song. Invariably at some point he sang 'Galway Bay', and dwelt long and lovingly on the words 'The strangers came and tried to teach us their way, but they might as well go chasing after moonbeams or light a penny candle for a star' — except that he changed 'the strangers' to 'the English'. The Protestants would laugh at Paddy's dislike of the English, but if he had tried to argue seriously for his point of view it would have ended in a brawl. Paddy may have been a Catholic but he was humorous and well liked, and that made all the difference. The reverse was true of the somewhat extreme Ulster Protestant who also worked with us. He was an Evangelical, very dogmatic and given to correcting people when opportunity arose (his brother, who had been a missionary in China, was not like that). It struck me at the time that if this chap was a Christian, it would be very difficult to make me one. The other members of the office staff impressed me with their hard work, ability and common sense. The senior people had a dry sense of humour and were kindly in dealing with our mistakes. One of my colleagues, who eventually emigrated to his uncle's sheep farm in Australia, came from a notorious part of Belfast called 'Tiger's Bay'; apparently they were 'tiger-like' in their dealings with the Catholics, whom they baited and taunted whenever they got the chance.

In my late teens I began to take religion more seriously, having come under the influence of a fiery Welsh preacher, whose sermons rang with passion and energy. A friend had taken me to his church (Presbyterian) which was puritanical in its austerity, following in a line of Presbyterian tradition. There was no organ, the box pews were hard and upright, and only psalms were sung. They were sung with great fervour, and it was somewhat ironical that hymn tunes were often used. In these unlikely surroundings I passed through a religious experience and decided to study for the Christian ministry. Much has been written about religious experience: its nature, validity and extent. But at that time it involved for me a commitment to the Christian faith that produced a sense of purpose and determination to try and succeed in living the Christian life. However, the way ahead appeared bleak. It was six years since I had been at school, and the subjects for matriculation appeared formidable: Latin, Greek, Mathematics, Physics, English, History. What was needed, I thought, was a tutor and a dedication to study which might gain me university entrance within a short time.

My tutor was the right kind of man for the job, but his fanaticism would have tried the patience of a saint. He was huge, angular and florid; quite pleasant at first meeting but turning into a tyrant once the teaching began. He would run through Latin verbs at great speed and was never satisfied until you could do the same. When the homework was brought he would peer at it and then take his pencil and, with a savage thrust that penetrated the paper, shout 'You didn't learn it, go back to the beginning!' He was a staunch believer in learning a subject thoroughly and would never have dreamed of changing his methods in the light of modern research. He was equally unchangeable in his religion and politics. If something was British it was good, so one knew how he felt about the Republic.

Having matriculated, I went up to Magee College, Derry, and met those students for the ministry with whom I was to live and study for four years. Some had come straight from school but many, like myself, had been in work of different kinds before matriculating. Some entered the teaching profession, but most decided for the parish ministry. There were no Catholics at Magee, which was a Presbyterian foundation; it only widened its scope in later years. But, as we shall see later, it figured in the dispute over the siting of the new University of Ulster at Coleraine. Many Catholics and Protestants of Derry argued strongly in favour of the development of Magee into a university, and it was alleged that obvious discrimination was shown in not doing this, based on the fear that it would become a Catholic stronghold.

There were two Christian societies at Magee: the conservative Evangelical Union and the much more liberal Student Christian Movement. The liberals joked about the Evangelicals, describing them as those who did not smoke, drink, dance or 'play with the girls'. The Evangelicals mourned the lack of true conversion in the liberals and their departure from the principles of the Reformed Faith. Evangelicals were in the majority, and they have always had a tremendous influence on Ulster Protestantism that the outsider finds difficult to understand. It is puritanical, stresses conversion, inclines to a fundamentalist view of the Bible, holds rigid ideas about the observance of the Sabbath, and keeps careful watch over the behaviour of members of the group. But there was little friction between the Evangelicals and liberals as long as theological debate was avoided, and they combined happily in both study and sport. All were studying for an Arts degree for which theology was not a subject (it was studied at post-graduate level), but we did receive some lectures on the interpretation of the Bible. This involved interpretation of the creation stories in Genesis, and because it opened up the conflict between religion and science, it came as something of a shock. The liberals did not find difficulty in accepting mythical interpretations, but it caused a heated debate among the Evangelicals. Some said they would never accept modern views which treated the Genesis stories as myths, while others hastily looked around for conservative arguments against such a view. Even at this stage, students were dividing into the 'closed mind' and the 'open mind' groups. I was excited by the debate and determined to pursue such problems at a later stage.

But here is an Ulster trait that is one of the reasons for the current unrest: minds which are closed to modern theological and political ideas. I was to meet people of this type so often in the course of my ministry in the Church. They could use the most modern equipment on their farms and in business, but in theology and politics they held on to what was outworn. In religion they kept stressing 'mystery' and 'faith', and these are indeed important aspects. But sometimes I had the suspicion that the word 'faith' was used as an excuse for an unwillingness to examine what they believed or perhaps to cover up a fear that they might be wrong. As a small boy said when asked for his definition of that word, 'faith is believing something which you know isn't true.' In politics they were Unionists and could never see any advantage in a united Ireland.

Derry itself, famed in the history of Ulster, did not really impress me. Many of the streets are narrow, it is hilly, and the walls which surround it gave me a feeling of being trapped. This was aggravated by my thinking that students for the ministry should study with those reading different subjects and going into other professions. I was glad to escape for the parts of the course which were taken at Trinity College. Dublin is a splendid city with wide, graceful streets, beautiful parks and Georgian mansions. The city was full of bicycles that travelled in Irish fashion four abreast amid the hooting of motor-cars which could not get past. It is near seaside resorts like Dun Laoghaire and Bray, and in those days you could take the old tram up to the top of Howth Head. One day we did just that, laughing and joking about the ability of the tram to make it, when the old conductor, noticing our Northern accents, growled: 'I know where you lot should be — back in the Black North.' The remark was unexpected and in contrast to the friendliness shown us by most Dubliners we met. I had a suspicion that he was one of the 'old guard' who might even have been involved in the I.R.A. at some time. Obviously he felt that no good thing could come out of Northern Ireland.

We lodged with Protestants and some of them complained of the treatment they received in the South and felt that Catholics were preferred to them when it came to getting jobs. To support this they pointed to the number of Protestants who had emigrated to other parts, but of course the emigration of Southern Catholics to mainland Britain and elsewhere is also very high. On Sundays crowds of people poured in and out of the Catholic churches; I had never seen so many people going to church before. One colleague joked, 'Those Italians were great missionaries.' Some Protestant Evangelical groups work in the South trying to convert the people to the true faith, as they say, but the results of such efforts are meagre. In those summer terms Dublin was gay, cosmopolitan, and free and easy. But I did not understand the Gaelic language, the culture or the sport. They played hurling and Gaelic football, which resembles rugby or American football, with the players handling the ball.

Having graduated from Trinity, I went to Princeton in the United States for further studies in theology. I look back on this as a good decision because it opened up my mind to the world at large and the great variety of interpretation and understanding of the Christian faith. But only two of us went out of a large group. Some went to New College in Edinburgh, but most remained at home in Ulster for their entire theological course of three years. This seems to me a mistake: 'Who Ireland knows that only Ireland knows?' Princeton seminary is the largest in the United States and draws students from all over the country and the world. The teaching was dominated by Scots: the President, the professor of church history, and the professor of systematic theology. It might be added that at parties they are easily persuaded to talk and sing; the latter is much appreciated by Americans, especially if they are clad in the kilt, and usually it consists of memories of the 'auld country' or the singing of '*The Hills of Home*'. I was accepted as Scotch-Irish, which is the way the Americans have of distinguishing the Northern from the Southern Irish. The Scotch-Irish were known for their hard work and determination, and for having supplied a number of American Presidents.* Both the Scots and the American members of staff were good teachers, and it was there that I was initiated into the mysteries of the *Westminster Confession of Faith* (1643), which I would be called upon to sign before ordination in the Presbyterian Church of Ireland. The teachers were critical of it, especially the clauses regarding predestination (God has chosen a certain number for life and ordained others for death) and its strong condemnation of the Pope. The view that came across was that if we had to sign it, we could do so with mental reservations. The Church historian was an excitable Scot who lectured very quickly and marched up and down as he did so. We were regaled with jokes as he took us through the history of the Churches. The Reformation, he said, was caused in Germany by Martin Luther wanting a wife, and in England by Henry VIII wanting to get rid of one. The

---

* The number is not inconsiderable: Chester Alan Arthur, James Buchanan, Grover Cleveland, Ulysses S. Grant, Benjamin Harrison, Andrew Jackson, Andrew Johnson, William McKinley, James Polk, Woodrow Wilson.

Anglican Church had a great variety of expression and was divided into three groups of churchmen: the High who wondered why at times they were not in the Catholic Church, the Broad who speculated so much about theology that they eventually had little of it left, and the Low Evangelical who put the stress on faith rather than works — in short, the High and hazy, the Broad and crazy, and the Low and lazy. While this man demonstrated that Church history need not be boring, what was entering my mind at the same time was the need to recognise variety and be tolerant of views different from my own.

I would definitely have stayed in America if my father had not died suddenly, with the result that I was called home; it seemed to me to be not only big but wide-open in opportunity. I had been assistant at a church in Chester, Pennsylvania, for a short time and liked the response of the young people and the businesslike way the affairs were conducted. However, my first assistantship in Ulster was right in the heart of ultra-Protestantism: the Shankill Road in Belfast. As I wandered from house to house encouraging the families to come to church I was greeted with friendliness, cups of tea, and witticisms. Some of the houses were painted red, white and blue, as were the pavements. On one of my breaks from Magee I had taught in a school in the area, so I knew something of the children. The level of education of both parent and child was low and they had only the haziest of ideas — a mixture of politics and religion — of what divided them from the Catholics. Usually they argued that the Catholics worshipped images, thought that the mass was something magical, and were ruled from the Vatican City. They knew little about the South and generally regarded it as a foreign country. Their houses were kept like 'little palaces' — extremely clean and tidy — and the pictures of the Royal Family on the walls were always carefully dusted. They called the minister whom I assisted 'Frosty' because he was not warm and informal as they were. Many belonged to the Orange Order and I noted that they came in full force for the Order's special services, but did not otherwise attend church regularly. In those days, fortunately, apart from threats and baiting of Catholics, there was not the disturbance later created by the troubles, but this was looming nearer.

My second assistantship was a complete contrast: a beautiful seaside resort which was also a prosperous dormitory town for Belfast. Here were moderate liberal Protestants drawn largely from the professional class, many of whom were to become members of the Alliance Party when the troubles came. This party was composed of both Catholics and

Protestants, and it sought to heal the divisions in the community. The town, apart from some explosions that broke shop windows in the main street, never experienced anything like the violence and turmoil that was to erupt on the Shankill Road. The people were kindly and tolerant, and endured with fortitude the somewhat long sermons given by the minister. At one session meeting, an elder became quite excited about this and exclaimed, 'Do you realise, minister, that the people have got to leave in order to get to the public conveniences?' He had meant to say 'public conveyances'.

From there I moved to my first ministry — again a complete contrast. I had been brought up near Belfast, worked there in business and had very little experience of farming or the country, but my first churches (joint-charge) were in the 'bandit country' of County Armagh. The locals referred to the place as 'the apple-breasted uplands' but as my wife and I travelled along the winding lanes to isolated farmhouses, we felt that we were in a foreign country. One of the churches had a number of upper-class farmers, who were very tolerant and kind. Its name was Lislooney, and when the minister with whom I had been assistant announced to the congregation that I was moving there his statement was misheard as 'He's gone looney.' I sometimes wondered later whether the latter interpretation was not more correct, but it was an experience not to be missed, for the farming community in Ulster forms a large part of the population and it enabled me to gain a knowledge of the way they thought. Some of them had never travelled as far as Belfast, and their centre of interest was the local community. We decided that the smaller church needed renovating, and embarked upon a series of concerts, sales of work and suchlike to bring in the money. The congregation worked hard and subscribed to gifts for the Church. There was one prominent member who reflected the Ulster trait of 'no change' by insisting exactly where the new pulpit had to be. Put the Irish way, he 'didn't care where it was as long as it was in the centre'. The theological reason was that in the Reformed tradition preaching was central, and so naturally that was where the pulpit had to be. He also insisted that the new notice-board should read, not 'church' but 'place of worship'. As far as I knew, this made the congregation unique because I could think of no other church that so named itself, not even in Ulster. This man was at loggerheads with another leading elder, and I had to spend a lot of time trying to bring them together since this set a poor example.

For this reason I visited him on a number of occasions and found that he feared modernity on his farm as well as in the Church. He refused to make use of tractors, and when I arrived he introduced me to his horses before his wife. When I said I liked horses he immediately prepared a mount for me to ride and nodded approvingly even when I showed signs of falling off. He was well versed in the scriptures, especially the Old Testament which like a rabbi he seemed to know by heart, and he never tired of telling me of sermons which he remembered even though they had been preached thirty years before. He recalled my predecessor — noted for his humour who had said before leaving the church that he had gathered all his sermons together and burned them: 'They burned well, they were very dry.' At one meeting of the Kirk session the old elder treated with scorn certain 'English ideas' about change which had been recently put forward in a joint meeting between Anglicans and Presbyterians. They had been introduced by an Anglican cleric who had spent much of his ministry in England. The elder rejected these ideas not only because they were new, but because they were 'foreign'. I pondered this cynically on my way home. Ulster was a country dependent economically on the British taxpayer and determined to remain in the United Kingdom, yet many of its population, like the old elder, refused any fresh ideas from the mainland, either political or religious.

At the opposite end of the scale there was that distinguished and pleasant Orangeman and Speaker in the Ulster parliament, Sir Norman Stronge, whom we visited a number of times at his home, Tynan Abbey. He belonged to the Anglican Ascendancy, which we will mention later. I was invited to attend meetings of the Orange Order as a minister, and he once humorously draped the sash over my shoulder and urged me to join (I never did), but he was much broader in his ideas than what the Order represented. To him, as to many like him, Orangeism was undoubtedly complementary to loyalty to the Union. One of the most tragic events in the troubles was his murder and that of his son by the I.R.A. The purpose of this atrocity is unfathomable, but in it Ulster lost one of her best representatives.

In general the level of education and knowledge of the world was low. Politics and religion were mixed together to such an extent that people no longer seemed to recognise the difference. One old chap whom I visited received me with the suspicion reserved for the stranger, but warmed as the conversation proceeded. He had a harsh, high-pitched voice that was difficult to listen to but as I left he assured me that though he had defected to the Catholics in times past (he had married one), he was thinking of coming back to the Protestant fold. As he put it: 'Though I am worshipping idols at the moment, I haven't forgotten

Billy.' The sexton of one of the churches appeared to be confused about the nature of the body after death. He complained that the dead bodies had been placed on a slope in the graveyard. 'Could you imagine anything worse', he said seriously, 'than lying there with the blood running towards the head?' I shook my head and wondered how such people would ever be able to distinguish fact from fiction or could escape the indoctrination of the preacher or politician who wanted to use them for his own ends.

At this point I naturally come to Paisley. He was just making a name for himself as an Evangelical preacher in a country that had been so saturated by missions, open-air preaching, American evangelism and so on, that Billy Graham refused to come to Ulster, pointing out that the need was much greater elsewhere. Every year I used to attend the Keswick Convention at Portstewart which cut across denominational barriers and consisted of people from all over Ireland and from the mainland. One year, Paisley and some of his ministers suddenly arrived at the hotel where we were staying and proceeded to disturb everybody by loud singing, preaching and praying. Did they think the Almighty was deaf? They behaved in the same way in the meetings of the Convention, much to the annoyance of the dignified chairman who later became Moderator of the Presbyterian Church. At that stage Paisley and his group of Free Presbyterian ministers (his church was just starting by encouraging people to leave their own churches, which he accused of 'not preaching the Gospel'), with their clownish ways, were not taken seriously, and had it not been for the troubles it is doubtful if he would have become a politician and gained his later notoriety. There was one member of their group whom I knew and had always considered a sensible person. He had joined Paisley after some years of training at a Bible college, but he seemed out of place amid all the clowning. I once told him of my amazement that Paisley in his church magazine was attacking sincere Evangelicals, especially Martin Smyth, who had been at university with me, as 'unsound' theologically or politically. He really had no answer, and it is significant to note that Smyth later became a staunch Ulster Loyalist and Grand Master of the Orange Order, which he could not have done had he been 'unsound' as Paisley alleged. But even though he and Paisley were to share this ultra-Loyalist stance, the two have never really agreed.

Paisley, like other more sinister twentieth-century demagogues, owes his rise to fame to his gifts as an orator, his ability to play on emotions and confirm prejudices, and his awareness of how the working class are thinking. He saw that to ally politics to religion was the way forward, and he took his message to the streets where his massive physique stood him in good stead. Paisley is not like a scholar, who weighs evidence for and against; instead he is dogmatic. He does not care whom he attacks, no matter how eminent for their spirituality, and some of the most fervent Evangelicals in all the Churches have come under his scathing tongue. He refuses to spare anyone who disagrees with him. Unfortunately, many of the people who listen to him do not have the education to see the one-sidedness of his arguments and many, being of the same opinion, rejoice in having their own views reinforced.

After three years we moved to a large church in Newry, a country town very near to the border with the Republic. This town is clearly divided into Catholic and Protestant areas. A clock and a sort of square mark the dividing line, and this place has been the scene of a very ugly confrontation between the two groups during the troubles. Our Church in the past had experienced a split because some members felt that they could not subscribe to the *Westminster Confession of Faith*. We shall consider this division later, but it was significant that the Non-Subscribing church (a beautiful building with a spire and white marble pulpit) was located in the Catholic quarter, for these Presbyterians in the nineteenth century had tended to side with the Catholics and sympathised with their complaints. Unlike the Evangelicals they stressed reason, and they could not accept the orthodox explanation of the doctrine of the Trinity. Sympathy might have been extended to them, but instead they were forced out of the main Presbyterian body by being asked to subscribe to the doctrine.

The church where I ministered was made up of bankers, teachers, lawyers, shopkeepers, civil servants, doctors and other middle-class people, and they were a very receptive and good-natured people. Since the community as a whole was largely Catholic, I was involved in town committees and met many of them. They were good-hearted and co-operative as long as what was proposed did not run counter to their political and religious beliefs. One remarked to me that he hoped for a united Ireland but on condition that the 'benefits' continued — he meant the welfare state, which supported the large Catholic families, but he was also thinking of the subsidies that were received by the farmers. He realised that economics was as important as politics. Another joked that there was a movement in the South to remove the inscription 'R.I.P.' (rest in peace) from all gravestones since they were the initials of a well-known Ulster preacher noted for his anti-Catholic sermons.

I belonged to the governing body of a number of state schools where all the pupils were Protestant. On one occasion the unusual happened: a Catholic applied to be appointed to the staff of one of them. He did not have a chance, of course, since the governors were all Protestants, and even if his qualifications had been outstanding (which they were not) he could not have been appointed because the parents would have refused to let him teach their children. I was responsible for religious education in the school while I was there, and noted that the children were able to learn a lot in a short time. But even the older ones could not apply the meaning of a scripture story to their own society. For example, I pointed out from the story of the good Samaritan that we were to love our neighbours, and that Jesus was trying to overcome racial and religious barriers between Jews and Samaritans. Thus he made the Samaritan the hero of the story, which must have caused offence to the Jews who listened. I mentioned that their neighbours were Catholics, whom they should also love, but this was received in stony silence. Apparently it was not what they had been told by their parents. Still it behoved the Protestants in the town to have at least a superficial friendliness with the Catholics, if only because the latter were in the majority. I noted this one evening at a church committee meeting. Usually everyone joined in a discussion, and it was difficult to bring the meeting to a close. But this evening I introduced the problem of one of our members who, I thought, was being asked to pay too much for the nursing she was receiving in a Catholic hospital. I said that we should go and protest about this to the church authorities. Imagine my surprise when some apologised and said that they had other appointments, and others remarked that she had plenty of money and could well afford it. Good relationships had to be maintained at all cost!

They also feared 'mixed marriages'. I sympathised with a young couple who were very much in love and wanted to marry, but the girl was a Presbyterian and the boy a Catholic. The parents of the girl were members of my church and pointed out that his church would insist on the marriage being performed by the priest and they would have to promise to bring their children up as Catholics. I argued with them, saying that he was not a very good Catholic and he might be persuaded to marry in our church; the couple could then choose for themselves the faith in which to rear the children. But the parents accused me of being against them and on the side of the Catholics, and left my church immediately.

Education was separate and so was housing. The Protestants lived in the best areas and branded as a traitor anyone who sold his house to a Catholic. The seller might plead that he could get much more money for the house from a Catholic, but he would be accused of selling his 'birthright for a mess of pottage'. Religious allegiance had to triumph over economics. As a Protestant you purchased your goods from Protestant shops, even though better and cheaper wares might be had in the Catholic quarter. Everybody knew that the dentists were better in the Catholic quarter, but you had to endure the pain inflicted by the Protestant 'tooth-puller'. Attendance by Protestants at Catholic services was ruled out, and when some of the local Protestant ministers tried to get together with the priests for a theological discussion, the Presbytery hauled them over the coals.

The clerk of the Presbytery was an old chap well past retiring age, and when he first met me he emphasised, 'Resist all change.' Once, when the Assembly suggested that men of his age might retire, he showed how fit he was by racing to the rostrum and protesting vigorously. At one meeting his Kirk Session suggested that a microphone and loudspeaker system might be installed in the church since the congregation had difficulty in hearing him. The meeting was being held in a small room and he rose to oppose such an idea: 'When such a thing is necessary,' he said, 'I will retire forthwith.' It was reported afterwards that despite the small size of the room, those in the back row had not heard him. His house was full of the minutes of the General Assembly (the supreme court of the Church that meets annually), which could have been a fire hazard, but he would not consent to their removal, despite his wife's pleading. The past was too precious, and all records had to be preserved, even at a risk to oneself. But he was kindly, very alert for his age, and the dispenser of a lot of good advice.

Orangeism was very strong in this part of the country, and there was a network of lodges which had frequent meetings to arrange for church parades and the celebration of days like the Twelfth. Many members of the congregations that I served were enrolled in the 'B Specials', and this force was accused by the Catholics of partisanship. But in those days, as far as I could see, they simply patrolled the roads at night and helped the police to keep law and order. They were a voluntary organisation and we shall say more about them later.

I attended a number of political meetings during my ministry, but became somewhat bored with the Unionist approach. While social conditions and the need to deal with unemployment were mentioned from time to time, there was virtually no mention of those grievances the

Catholics had concerning votes in local elections, discrimination over housing and employment, and lack of development in Catholic areas. The main burden of the speeches was how to preserve the link with Britain and prevent the Republic of Ireland from interfering in the affairs of Ulster. Fear was expressed that a future Labour government coming to power in Britain might move away from the Acts which stated that Ulster would remain part of the United Kingdom unless the majority of the people there desired otherwise. On one occasion I was present at a meeting where a member of my church was campaigning for election and suddenly found myself called upon to speak by a Unionist politician who had been strongly advocating the need for the Churches to support Unionism. I was somewhat taken back, not having prepared a speech, but I noted that when I mentioned that we had a Protestant parliament at Stormont, this was greeted with loud cheers. However, when I insisted that the Church must be the conscience of the state and seek to resolve differences and protest against discrimination in its various forms, there was an eloquent silence accompanied by a certain restlessness. It struck me then that there were certain things that Protestants wanted to hear and if a speaker stressed them — union with Britain, Protestantism, the battle of the Boyne, the siege of Derry, the British way of life and so on — he was popular and could win the support of the electorate. It was a great shock to Protestants in the North of Ireland when, as we see below (p. 68 ff.), a politician emerged as leader of the Unionist Party who wanted to move in the direction of reform of their society, and tried to break down the traditional barriers between Catholic and Protestant. Thus Terence O'Neill was to split the Unionist Party and arouse the expectations of Catholics, so that they took to the streets in the Civil Rights Association to demand a faster pace of change.

I had been in the ministry for eight years, plus three as an assistant, when my mother died and I felt free to accept an appointment as senior lecturer in the Department of Philosophy and Religion in the University of Ife, Nigeria. On the ship travelling to Lagos I met an Ulster Catholic, a graduate of Queen's University, Belfast, who was in the oil business. He treated me like one of his priests and discussed not only discrimination but his personal problems. The following year he came all the way to Ife from Lagos over a bumpy and partly unsurfaced road to see us. I also met two Irish nuns on the ship who were going to work as missionaries. Once while I was having a friendly conversation with them, the news came over the ship's radio that an ecumenical service in St Anne's Cathedral, Belfast, had been disrupted by Mr Paisley. Nigeria was in the grip of civil war, but fortunately we were in the West and saw little of it. I gave lectures in philosophy and theology to large classes of students who professed a wide variety of faiths. There were Catholics and Protestants, but they were in the minority compared with the Muslims and adherents of African traditional religion. The staff of the department included a Muslim, a Jesuit priest, a Jew, an Anglican Nigerian and a Presbyterian. From this angle the divisions of Ulster appeared less important.

After three years we returned to England and spent six happy years with the Geordies in the North-East. They were warm and friendly, just like the Ulster people, but did not distinguish between the North and South of Ireland, and had never heard of the difference brought about by the plantation of settlers in the North which will be described in the next chapter. They could not understand what the fighting in the province was about. They lived happily with their Roman Catholic neighbours, and differences in worship and theology did not interest them. They were more concerned about the relation of science to religion, and how religion could justify itself in a secular age. In 1974 we moved to the south of England and found the same thing. The people there considered that to fight about religion in a scientific and pluralistic age was crazy. It was illogical — it was 'Irish'. But sympathy was expressed with the Catholics, who appeared to them to be oppressed by bigoted Ulster Protestants living in the past and speaking dogmatically with harsh accents that made what they said even more difficult to understand. It is to try and remove some of this lack of understanding that I have written the following chapters.

2
THE HISTORICAL FACTOR

It is difficult to separate the historical and religious factors which have led to the present impasse in Ulster, but in order to clarify the situation as much as possible, an attempt will be made in this chapter to do so. It is admitted that the two factors often overlap, but an emphasis on the historical will bring the religious dimension into sharper focus in Chapter 3. No attempt is made here to write a history of Ulster, which has been very well done by others, but to select events and actions which may point to the way in which the character of the province has been moulded.

Ulster is a beautiful country, and what makes it beautiful — its mountains, glens, lakes and coasts — has formed a natural barrier to the progress of any invader. Even when the Normans in the South were ruthlessly looting, pillaging and building their castles, the Irish kings of Ulster continued to rule their territory undisturbed by the Norman power. These O'Neills inspired a remarkable loyalty and devotion in their warlike subjects, and while the successive invaders — Norsemen, Vikings, Normans — made certain inroads into Ulster, it was of small significance compared with what they accomplished in the South. It is true that Niall More O'Neill paid homage to Richard II, but nevertheless he remained the ruler of the North.[1] The English tried in the sixteenth century to bring this wild land under control, sometimes by invasion and sometimes by diplomacy, but the O'Neills continued to be a thorn in their flesh. One of them dared to invade the 'English Pale', the district around Dublin settled by the English; and, despite the protests of Elizabeth I, Shane O'Neill ruled independently.

A different way of taming 'the O'Neill' (a mystical title, regarded with awe and reverence by the inhabitants of Ulster) was tried by Elizabeth when she brought Shane's younger brother Hugh to London to be educated in English ways and manners.[2] He soon became acquainted with the arts of war, diplomacy, politics and statecraft, and had access to the court; but this training could not remove the feeling of independence which was in his blood, and only helped him to understand the best way of waging war known to his contemporaries. Thus he became the first Irish leader to bring into the field an army disciplined and equipped to meet an English regiment on equal terms. He took the title 'the O'Neill', and with thousands of Irish and Scottish soldiers defeated an English force at Clontibret in 1595. Victory after victory followed, and England, worried about possible alliances of Hugh with Spain and Scotland, sent the largest army possible to destroy him. But the Earl of Essex who was in command concluded a truce with Hugh, much to the displeasure of Elizabeth, who was forced to send in an even greater army under Mountjoy. Hence, Hugh was only defeated by extraordinary efforts on the part of the English and by pouring men and money into the country on an unprecedented scale.[3] This warlike trait continued in Ulster, and it was James I who determined to change it by introducing Scottish and English settlers into the country. Henceforth the two were to be combined under the title: the Ulster Scot. This plantation was to become a decisive factor for the future not only of the North but of the country as a whole.

Hugh O'Neill had submitted to the Crown in 1603, and received a pardon. He had also been allowed to retain his lands in Ulster, much to the annoyance of the English officers who had fought against him for years. But O'Neill's warlike spirit could not be content with the reduction of his rights as 'the O'Neill', and he suffered continual harassment from the English who enforced the terms of the submission and penalised him because he was a Catholic. Hence he and his ally the Earl of Tyrconnell took flight in 1607 on a French ship bound for Europe. This came as a great surprise to England, although it had long been suspected that he was involved in a plot with Spain.

This gave the English Crown the opportunity, long awaited, to deprive the native landlords of their estates, and great areas were handed over to English and Lowland Scottish settlers — but, contrary to the government's intention, there was no large-scale removal of the native population.[4] The big question was the allocation of land, and there were some 500,000 acres to be disposed of. The settlers were required to take the Oath of Supremacy, recognising the King as head of the Church. The Irish natives were not required to take the oath, and as their share they received only about 58,000 acres. The native gentry fared worst of all in this, for the best land passed from them to the settlers.[5] Thus this plantation sowed the seeds of rebellion, not only because of the land confiscation but because it introduced a new race of people into the country. These ethnic, cultural and religious differences lie at the heart of the Ulster problem, and are not sufficiently understood.

The two counties of Antrim and Down had already been planted by Scots in 1603, but Monaghan under the settlement of 1590 was left to the Irish. The corporation of London in 1610 was heavily involved, and from this the county and city of Londonderry are named. The six counties of Armagh, Cavan, Coleraine (now Londonderry), Donegal,

Fermanagh and Tyrone were occupied. Thus a British and Protestant population was steadily built up, and it was reckoned that in 1641, of the 3,500,000 acres in the six counties, the Protestants owned 3,000,000 and the Catholics the rest. But, as Curtis notes, the proportion held by Catholics was to be further reduced after 1660, and after 1690 scarcely any of the Gaelic and Catholic aristocracy remained.[6] Hence we may speak of two plantations (1603 and 1610), the first composed of warlike Highlanders from the Western Islands and the second drawn from the Lowlanders and English. Like all emigrants they were brave, and they came to an unruly land which had proved ungovernable in the past.

What the settlers discovered as time passed was that the colonising was not total, for the native Irish had not been driven into the hills and bogs, as has often been said, but lived all around them. Resentful of the colonisers and quite understandably enraged by the loss of their land, they waited for the right moment to take revenge. The settlers were fully aware of this, and felt more like a beleaguered garrison surrounded by enemies than masters in their new homes.[7] Thus we see emerging the dominant characteristic of fear. The unknown is always dreaded, and if a proper integration of settlers and native Irish could have taken place, this would have been overcome. Instead the fear was fully justified and realised by the massacres of the colonists that took place in 1641.

In some ways it was the fault of the English government that a possible integration did not take place. The Scottish men, in particular, were very much inclined to marry Irish girls, and if this had been encouraged or even allowed, it would have gone some way to break down the barriers of culture, race and religion. But this was not only discouraged; it was actually punishable, because of the fear that the whole settlement would 'degenerate' into an Irish colony.[8] Such a policy had its inevitable result: rebellion. In November 1641, the Irish Catholics struck the first blow at Portadown where 100 settlers were killed in the most gruesome way. Some were shot, others drowned, and some even buried alive. The whole of Ireland was soon in ferment as Owen Roe O'Neill, nephew of the great Hugh, arrived from Spain to command the forces of both Gaelic Catholic and Old English (planters established in both the South and the North-East for several centuries). In the event it was estimated that 12,000 Protestants died either by murder or privation.[9] But the warlike spirit of the settlers had been aroused by the atrocities, and they successfully defended Carrickfergus (the ancient seat of power in Ulster), Belfast, Newry and Lisburn. Then General Robert Monro, commanding 2,500 Scots, put the rebellion down with terrible ferocity.

However, this severity was minor compared with what Cromwell did to the whole country. He passed like lightning through the land leaving a trail of massacre, burning, atrocity and banishment for those who had been involved in rebellion. Men, women and children were killed without mercy at Drogheda, Wexford and elsewhere; and all this was done, as he said, so that 'God alone should have all the glory.' Such a belief that he was the avenging angel of God 'left a mark and memory that succeeding centuries have not been able to wipe out'.[10] The Cromwellian settlement demanded loyalty from all Irish landlords, otherwise their estates would be forfeited, and a new and thorough plantation of the country was planned and carried through. Thus in 1641 it could be said that the majority of the landlords in Ireland had been Catholics before the Settlement, but they were now Protestants and the balance of power in the country was changed.[11] From this time on, Roman Catholics were regarded as not being loyal to England. Thus we see that the separation of colonists and native Irish, of Catholic and Protestant, was cemented and hardened by the events of the rebellion of 1641 and its tragic consequences. If hatred had become a characteristic of the Ulster Protestants, this was now fully reciprocated by the Catholics.

However, the Protestants' fear continued after the restoration of the monarchy in 1660. They watched anxiously as the restored king, Charles, II, freeing himself from parliamentary control, moved in the last years of his reign towards the establishment of an absolute and Catholic monarchy. But because Charles was not willing to disturb Protestants who had given him back his crown, the fear faded a little. However, it grew to alarm when the openly Catholic James II succeeded in 1685; he appointed Catholics to high offices of state in Ireland, and a Catholic-dominated Irish parliament passed an Act revoking the Cromwellian land settlement. In the face of this, Anglicans and Presbyterians in Ulster decided, for the time being as least, to forget their differences in face of the common danger to their position.[12]

Events now followed that developed another trait in the Ulster Protestant character: a feeling of superiority and ascendancy over the Catholic Irish. This flowed from the victory gained at the battle of the Boyne. James II, having alienated the English parliament and the majority of his British subjects, fled on 23 December 1688 to France where he received the protection of his cousin, Louis XIV. The Princess Mary and her husband William, Prince of Orange, succeeded her father James on the throne, and this was received with great joy and jubilation. But the province was alive with rumour and counter-rumour. A particular item of news was that a Catholic regiment was to be sent to

Londonderry to relieve the Protestant one which had garrisoned it previously. In Ulster the fear mounted that the soldiers would turn on them and that the 1641 massacres would be repeated. While the authorities hesitated over what to do next, thirteen apprentice boys took the law into their own hands, seized the keys to the city gates of Londonderry, and slammed the gates shut in the face of the arriving troops: Lord Antrim's Redshanks.

However, James — urged on by Louis, who was opposed to William's European plans for an anti-French alliance — made a final effort to recover his throne. He arrived in Ireland in March 1689, and his first act was to summon Parliament, where he was met with demands by the Catholic Irish to disown the Episcopal Church, confiscate the estates of over 2,000 Protestant landlords, and ensure that the English Parliament would not be able to bind Ireland. No wonder that James, disagreeing with a number of these proposals, complained that he was 'fallen into the hands of a people who rammed many hard things down his throat'.[13] In April, he proceeded to besiege Londonderry and cut the city off from the sea by placing across the river Foyle a boom made of beams studded with iron clamps and roped together. The English ships hesitated for some time when they saw this obstruction. The commander of the garrison, Lieutenant-Colonel Robert Lundy, overawed by the nearness of the royal presence, was in favour of surrendering the city to James, but his authority was set aside by the people, and he had to flee the city disguised as a common soldier with a load of matchwood on his back.[14] In commemoration of the event in later times, matchwood has been used to light the fires to burn Lundy in effigy.

The people in the city endured all kinds of hardships, but successfully repulsed the attacks of James who, fortunately for them, had no artillery. These 30,000 Ulstermen lived on dogs, cats, mice, candles and leather, but held out inspired by their commander Major Henry Baker and the Reverend George Walker, an Anglican clergyman. Robert Kee refers to the skirmishes that took place outside the walls and to a clever ruse planned by the commander of the besieging army. He rounded up thousands of Protestants from the neighbouring countryside and, driving them to a place out in the open in front of the walls, said that he would leave them without food and water until the town surrendered. The citizens retaliated by erecting a gallows up on the wall in full view of the besieging army, from which they said they would hang Catholic prisoners unless the wretched people below the walls were released. James II's commander had to give in.[15] It is little wonder that such a siege attracted European attention and is referred to by Beckett as 'the most famous siege in British history'. Finally, on 1 August 1689, the English ship *Mountjoy* broke through the boom and the siege was lifted. Thus today the apprentices are celebrated as heroes and Lundy's effigy is burned. To the defenders the ending of the siege seemed a miracle, since many of them were so weak with hunger and exhaustion that they could hardly stand upright.

William himself reached Ulster in August 1689 and defeated James at the Boyne. The Protestant supremacy of Ireland now began. It is somewhat ironical, when we think of the loyalty of Ulster today to the British Crown, that in this decisive battle and campaign the Catholics were led by an English king and the Protestants by a Dutch one. No Irish war has left such an indelible mark on the mind of Ulster as this one, and it is kept fresh by the annual parades in the country of the Orange Order and the Apprentice Boys of Belfast and Derry. In this war too, Ireland moved into the European stage of operations, for the native Irish were looking to France and often to Spain. Papal influence was apparent, and the Irish scene had become part of the greater plans for European conquest nurtured respectively by William of Orange and by Louis XIV of France.[16] From this time on, politics and religion are closely interwined in the history of Ireland. Throughout the eighteenth century, Catholics were discriminated against, but measures were also taken by the Irish parliament against Protestant dissent, and this had the effect of linking Presbyterians and Catholics together in a common cause. We shall look more closely at this in the next chapter.

Ulster was prospering at this time, having established a trade monopoly, and links with Scotland were jealously guarded. The position of farmers was better than in the rest of the country, for they had security of tenure. The linen industry was moving ahead strongly. Still, the North was as annoyed as the South by English restrictions on trade and by the absentee landlord system. This discontent among emigrants from Ulster in America helped to push the colonists along the path to complete independence. The Declaration of Independence itself is in the handwriting of an Ulsterman, and it was an Ulsterman who first printed it. Washington himself declared: 'If defeated everywhere I will take my last stand for liberty among the Scotch-Irish of my native Virginia.'[17] As we have already noted, several of his successors as President of the United States have been of Ulster descent.

Here we see a certain ambivalence in the Ulster character. On the one hand there was the loyalty to the English Crown arising from the

Plantation, but on the other hand a reaction against dependence because of the treatment they received. One explanation could be that the Scots, who formed the majority of the colonists, had contended for independence in their wars against England, and this reasserted itself among those who had settled in Ulster. Certainly there were signs that they were prepared to join not only the Protestants of the South but also the Catholics against the restrictions placed upon participation in trade and membership of Parliament. Thus we have the United Irishmen, founded in Belfast and Dublin in 1791, which derived much of its inspiration from the 'liberty' cry of the French Revolution. However, this unification was tempered by other societies, such as the Orange Order (founded in 1795) with its strong loyalty to the Crown.[18] It is important to note this streak of independence, for in the mid-1980s actual independence in the form of statehood has been asserted as a possibility in reaction to the British government's signing of an accord with Dublin. It also appeared at the time of the campaign for Irish Home Rule. However, two events conspired at this time to remove it from the minds of the Ulster Protestants: a failed insurrection organised by the United Irishmen, and the Act of Union of Great Britain and Ireland on 1 January 1801, creating a 'United Kingdom' with a single parliament.[19]

Daniel O'Connell, 'the Liberator' who paved the way for Catholic Emancipation in Great Britain and built up Irish nationalism in conjunction with the Catholic Church, tried to win over to his nationalist cause the last remnants of Protestant nationalism in the North, but he failed because of his alliance with the Catholics. He met his match in Henry Cooke, a Presbyterian minister, of whom we shall hear much more in the next chapter. Cooke rallied the Presbyterians, together with the Established Church, in defence of the Union.[20] The great tragedy of the potato famine, which took a vast toll of dead in the South, drove the thought of politics out of their minds. It did not have this effect on the North, not only because the North was less dependent on potatoes but also because of the great expansion of Ulster's industries at that time.[21] Thus the distinctive character of the North became even more strongly marked. But in the South a movement developed after the famine which, with its use of force, led the way to the modern Irish Republican Army, and which had dire consequences for the future of Ulster.

I remember my inability as a child in Ulster to understand the word 'Fenian'; I knew it only as a term of abuse. It originated from Fianna, a legendary band of warriors, and was the name of the movement in the South responsible for the risings of 1848 and 1867. There were Protestant members of this organisation like Smith O'Brien, John Mitchell (son of a Presbyterian minister) and James Stephens, and there were also Irish Catholics and Americans, both Catholic and Protestant. Although the early risings came to nothing, the Fenian rebellion of 1916 under Patrick Pearse led to national sovereignty and freedom from England.

It was the Home Rule issue which showed how distinctive Ulster was. Various reasons have been put forward why England was reluctant to grant Home Rule to Ireland and why it took three attempts before the Bill was successfully passed. One, perhaps, was English nationalism which recognised that Ireland was of vital strategic importance to Britain and useful as a 'food basket'. Such nationalism backed Ulster's opposition to Home Rule, based as it was on the fear of Catholicism, because Britain would lose the Ulster economy which was complementary to its own, being dependent on the mainland not only for markets but for supplies. Thus, during the struggle over the Home Rule bill of 1912, a Unionist postcard labelled 'Belfast under Home Rule' showed one of the principal streets overgrown with grass and a notice saying 'To Let' stuck up in front of the City Hall.[22]

Gladstone introduced the first Home Rule Bill in April 1886 despite the mounting tension in Ulster, where in August 1864 an effigy of Daniel O'Connell was burned and riots and conflicts between Protestant and Catholic workmen had continued over the previous twenty years. The Bill proposed that an Irish parliament be set up, although the Imperial legislature was to retain control over such vital matters as the army, the navy, ports and foreign affairs, and free trade was to be maintained between the two countries.[23] Gladstone had a parliamentary majority of 86 over the Conservatives, and he sought to please the Irish Nationalist members (led by Charles Stewart Parnell) in order to get the policies of his Liberal Party passed. The granting of Home Rule to Ireland would put them firmly on his side — or so he hoped. In his speech introducing the Home Rule Bill, he appeared to underestimate the strength of opposition in Ulster, referring to it as 'momentary ebullitions, which will pass away with the fears from which they spring'. Such fears he would do everything to assuage, but 'I cannot allow it to be said that a Protestant minority in Ulster, or elsewhere, is to rule the question at large for Ireland. . . .'[24]

One of his sharpest opponents was Lord Randolph Churchill, the father of Winston, and he unlike his son was determined to arouse the opposition of Ulster to the Bill. He spoke in the Ulster Hall to a huge and excited audience whom he urged to organise and prepare. And he uttered a phrase which was to become a slogan of the campaign and be repeated many times down the years: 'Ulster will fight and Ulster will be right.'²⁵ Opposing Churchill and supporting Gladstone was a Protestant: Charles Stewart Parnell, the leader of the Irish Nationalists. For those who think that the Ulster conflict resolves itself neatly into a conflict between Protestant and Catholic, the life of Parnell is a revealing study, although he came from Dublin and not from Ulster. Parnell also illustrates that independent streak in Protestantism which we have seen developing in the United Irishmen and which at first opposed the Union of the two countries but then supported it. But the independent streak in Parnell was strengthened by his mother, an American who held strongly to the Declaration of Independence and instilled this into her son. A Protestant landlord, owning some 5,000 acres in County Wicklow, he had been educated in England and had an English accent. This background was summed up by Michael Davitt in the well-known words, 'an Englishman of the strongest sort moulded for an Irish purpose'.²⁶

Although Parnell had contact with Fenians and members of the Irish Republican Brotherhood, he did not favour violence. However, at times, he came into conflict with Gladstone over speeches which implied that the only link between Ireland and England should be the Crown. He was imprisoned for that and other actions on behalf of tenant rights in Ireland. But he showed a fatal recklessness in his love for Katherine O'Shea. She was the wife of one of the Irish Members of Parliament, Captain O'Shea, whose need for money made him encourage the friendship. That liaison led to Parnell's downfall. The first Home Rule Bill was defeated by 343 votes to 313 in the House of Commons. Parnell, dogged by ill-health, lost one by-election after another, and died on 6 October 1891. On the Home Rule issue he was strongly opposed by the Orange Order, to which we now turn our attention.

The Orange Order, as we have seen, was founded in 1795, and one of its objectives was to keep alive the 'pious and immortal memory' of William III (Prince of Orange), the saviour of the Protestant religion in Ireland. It replaced such Protestant groups as the Orange Boys and the 'Peep O'Day Boys'. The latter were so called because they raided Catholic homes at dawn, and it was they who had figured so prominently in the conflict with the Catholic group known as the Defenders. The best known-battle between the Defenders of the Catholic rights and the 'Peep O'Day Boys' occurred near the town of Armagh in 1795 and was called the 'battle of the Diamond' after the crossroads where it took place. The Defenders seemed to have suffered worse in the skirmish than their opponents, for they eventually retired leaving thirty or forty of their number dead.

The Orange Order then brought the 'Peep O'Day Boys' and the various 'Orange Boy' societies under its wing, and marched in the first

'Glorious Twelfth' in 1797. According to a contemporary account, they marched in regular files by companies, unarmed, each carrying a flag. The flags were decorated with portraits, especially of King William, and slogans referring to his having finally established the Protestant religion. The marchers were quiet and sober, and numbered about 1,500.[27]

It is generally agreed that membership in the early stages was almost entirely Anglican and came from the lower strata of society, i.e. labourers and artisans. But within a year the numbers had reached 5,000 and members of the gentry and government were beginning to give it support (at one time it could boast the Earl of Enniskillen as its Grand Master) — this in spite of the fact that it continued the sectarian strife and tried to drive the Catholics from their homes. A typical slogan (originally ascribed to Cromwell) was uttered when a Catholic household was broken into in the early dawn: 'To hell or to Connaught!' Most Catholics needed no second telling and fled to the province of Connaught with all speed.

This violence was not consistent with the Christian religion which the members professed, but the movement continued to spread with the founding of lodges throughout the country, and even in Dublin people of position and influence joined the new lodge there in 1797. By 1830, as Liam de Paor points out, Orangeism had already evolved its potent myths: 'The plantation, the wilderness settled with Bible and sword, the massacres of 1641 and the martyrdom of the settlers by the treacherous and barbarous uprising of the natives; the threat to "freedom, religion and laws" caused by the accession of the popish James II, the glorious revolution which overthrew him, the sufferings, endurance, valour and triumph of the cause and Derry, Enniskillen, Aughrim and the Boyne. There were too the victories of the Diamond and other local affrays where the good Protestants, compassed by enemies, had prevailed and survived, being ultimately delivered, like God's chosen people in the Bible, from the hands of their enemies.'[28] Their general attitude to the Catholics was summarised in the slogan: 'Croppies [Catholics] lie down!' and this was usually followed by the song:

> *Poor Croppies, ye knew that your sentence was come*
> *When you heard the dread sound of the Protestant drum —*
> *In memory of William we hoisted his flag*
> *And soon the bright Orange put down the Green rag.*

It is little wonder that the government of the day had to arouse itself to put an end to such activity, and Thomas Drummond, the Under Secretary for Ireland, dissolved the Order in 1836. But it was only sleeping, not dead! After ten years it was revived, and again rioting and sectarian strife followed the marches of 1849, 1857, 1872, 1886, 1935 and 1969. The horrifying incidents which occurred on 12 August 1969 at the annual Apprentice Boys' march (to commemorate the Protestants who in 1688 shut the city gates of Derry against the army of James II) are still fresh in the minds of many people. In the days that followed, the confrontation between Catholics and Protestants spread throughout the country, with Protestants surging through Catholic areas of Belfast, firing guns, burning houses, shouting obscenities, plundering and looting. British troops were called to act as a buffer between the two sides, and erected a peace line, sometimes called the Orange-Green line, between the Falls Road and the Shankill Road.

The Orange Order thrives in times of crisis. Thus, having come to see the Act of Union in 1801 as a safeguard of their position, they organised opposition to O'Connell's campaign to have it repealed. Again, resistance to Home Rule injected the Order with new life and enabled it to recruit all classes to its ranks. At the time of the signing of the Covenant in 1912, it was licensed to engage in military activities; and many Orangemen subsequently demonstrated their loyalty to the Crown in a different but equally eloquent way at the battle of the Somme.

There seems to be no important area of life in the province of Ulster which the Order has not influenced. The Ulster Special Constabulary drew on it for recruits; it actively opposes ecumenical dialogue among the Churches; it has had an influence in maintaining the segregated system of education in the province, and up till 1969 any Unionist politician who hoped to be elected had to belong to the Order. In the light of the Order's activities it was somewhat puzzling to hear a prominent politician like Brian Faulkner speaking of tolerance as one of the fundamental tenets of Orangeism. Having admitted that in 1969 the Order expelled Phelim O'Neill, M.P., from its ranks because he had attended a Catholic funeral service, he said that this was unusual and probably due to the current tension in the country. He, as an Orangeman, together with other members, had often attended the funerals of Catholics and he had never known anyone to be expelled for it; but in a speech on the 'Twelfth' he had to remind the Orangemen that William of Orange was a liberal and enlightened monarch, and that this was what was meant by 'Remember 1690'.[29]

Faulkner seemed to have forgotten that among the qualifications for a member of the Order the following is laid down:

He should strenuously oppose the fatal errors and doctrines of the Church of

Rome and scrupulously avoid countenancing (by his presence or otherwise) any act or ceremony of Popish worship; he should, by all lawful means, resist the ascendancy of that church, its encroachments and the extension of its powers, ever abstaining from all uncharitable words, actions or sentiments towards his Roman Catholic brethren.[30]

Thus the Orangeman is not allowed to attend Catholic funerals or any other kind of service. This is a very negative requirement but, given that he believes the Catholic Church to be in error, it is also made entirely clear that he has no right to engage in unlawful attacks on its members. Further, he by no means lives up to the religious requirements, which are 'a sincere veneration for his Heavenly Father and a humble and steadfast faith in Jesus Christ'. If Church attendance is a sign of this faith, the Orangeman is deficient since he is usually there solely for parade services. Further, it is also required that he should cultivate 'brotherly kindness and charity, devotion and piety', and that 'his deportment should be gentle and compassionate, kind and courteous.'

Such requirements for membership as these are plainly Christian, but it is plain too that they are the sort of ideals to which no more than lip-service is necessary, for otherwise the hierarchy of the Order, in the light of the behaviour of many Orangemen since the troubles started in 1968, would need to engage in a mass expulsion of members. But they are not slow to express their disapproval of clergy who dare to criticise them. Eric Gallagher has written of how he incurred this disapproval when he dared to speak of religious apartheid. He demanded to know how clergy could remain in such an institution, and whether they should encourage Orangemen in their congregations to resign. Should moderates in the Order not challenge it to live up to its professed aims and ideals? Certainly, Gallagher has concluded, the Orange Order articulates the fears of the majority in such a way as to suggest that they can only go the way of obstinate resistance rather than seeking mutual accommodation. Thus it is an obstacle to peace.[31]

However, in those crisis days of the Home Rule proposals from 1886 onwards, the Order was viewed as a suitable partner for Ulster Unionism, which itself was rapidly developing with a network of societies and clubs in towns throughout Ulster. But it was not till 1905 that the Ulster Unionist Council united all these Unionists associations. This unification was to provide strong opposition to the third Home Rule Bill.

There was a threat of civil war in Ulster during the debates over the second Home Rule Bill of 1892, and it was reported that an army was being formed to resist Home Rule. At a great Convention organised by the Unionists in Belfast, about 12,000 people cheered with wild enthusiasm as speaker after speaker declared, 'We will not have Home Rule.' In the House of Lords there was stiff opposition to the Bill, and doubts were expressed about the British army being prepared to shoot Ulster loyalists. Thus when the Bill was passed in the House of Commons, the House of Lords threw it out, by 419 to 41 votes. It has long been standard advice to politicians in England that they should avoid the Irish problem, since so many have found it the graveyard of their hopes. Gladstone was no exception to this. His advocacy of the Irish cause proved 'disastrous for his party, and from 1886 to 1906, save for an interval of three years, was effective in putting all the Conservative elements into power.'[32]

These events demonstrated the traits of the Ulster Protestants' outlook which we have already noted: warlike pride in the Protestant ascendancy, loyalty to the Crown, and a streak of independence aroused by what is seen as unfair treatment. Now, as a new crisis over Home Rule loomed, outright defiance became a strong characteristic. The leading actors in this drama, especially on the Ulster stage, were to become legendary figures, and two in particular need our attention: Sir Edward Carson and Captain James Craig, respectively the leader and the organiser of the resistance. When the Liberals under H.H. Asquith were returned to power and made preparations to introduce the third Home Rule Bill, Craig approached Carson and asked him to lead the Unionists. Carson was a Dublin barrister who had never taken a case until he was sure not only of his client but that there was a good chance of winning. He wanted to know whether the Ulster people were really in earnest and willing to fight. Craig therefore organised a demonstration, consisting of some 50,000 Orangemen and Unionists who paraded to his home at Craigavon, near Belfast. When Carson saw the vast crowd, he realised that they really did mean to resist and that it was not, as many politicians in England believed, a game of bluff. He addressed them and said: 'With the help of God, you and I joined together . . . will yet defeat the most nefarious conspiracy that has ever been hatched against a free people.' Compared with Paisley, Carson was far from being an emotional rabblerouser. From humble beginnings he had attained the position of (Conservative) Solicitor-General by hard work, intelligence and skill. He had brought the unfortunate Oscar Wilde down by ruthless cross-examination, and figured in the case of the naval cadet Archer-Shee accused of stealing a five shilling postal order, when he proved the

Admiralty wrong.[33] It is hard to understand how he came to embrace the Ulster cause. He had been born in Dublin, and even spoke with a Southern accent. Perhaps it was his Presbyterian background, or his feeling that injustice was being done, or a conviction that Ireland could not prosper if she were ever separated from England. But, once committed, he was determined to see it through to the end.

James Craig was the millionaire director of a whiskey firm, and it is to him that we look for our next Ulster characteristic. He lived on the farm at Craigavon where he was born on 8 June 1871, and grew up as a cheerful average boy, with the distinctive view that he was an Ulsterman and not Irish. In 1906 he won the East Down parliamentary seat, and tried to improve education in the country. He was Presbyterian but not anti-Catholic, and wanted integrated schooling in order to break down social barriers. Possessing a sharp wit and an enquiring mind, he did not allow criticism in parliament to deter him. In 1911, as we have seen, his rebellious nature became evident when he organised a protest march of 50,000 against Home Rule and defied the government in the House of Commons. He set up the Ulster Volunteers and a provisional administration in case Home Rule were to become a reality, and organised clandestine gun-running to Ulster from the continent of Europe. However, once the danger point was passed, he showed his loyalty to the Crown during the Great War and, as the recognised leader of the Loyalists, was even able to offer conscription in Ulster to win Westminster's support.

The fact that he came from farming stock was a tremendous advantage to him in a largely agricultural community. People felt that he talked their language, and he was often in the streets of Belfast and other towns in order to meet them.[34] From Craig's tolerance towards the Catholics and much else the question arises: did being a Protestant not mean for him simply loyalty to the Empire, the Crown, and the Act of Union with Britain, rather than a religious difference from Catholics so deep as to be unbridgeable? It would appear that any Catholic who shared these loyalties was acceptable to him. We examine this question more fully in the next chapter since it is often taken for granted by those who write and comment on Ulster today that it is religious differences that separate the two communities in the province. But the evidence of history indicates that Ulster people can have an intense loyalty to the Crown and dislike of the Republic while being only loosely attached to the Christian faith. Craig represents the kind of tolerance that is usually found in people who have travelled and had a good education, and which was not shared by the majority of the Orangemen and Unionists whom he organised. In this final Home Rule crisis we see coming to the surface obstinacy, self-reliance, directness, strength and violence. Craig had his full share of some of these characteristics, but he was no religious bigot as many members of the Orange Order were.

The anger and violence of those days was the result of fear and mistrust. Religion was connected with the element of fear because it was shouted on the streets and printed in the newspapers that 'Home rule was Rome rule'. The mistrust was centred on the belief that the British government would not respect the fact that the Ulster people were British and loyal subjects, and would hand them over to an Irish parliament. They were, of course, proud of their Protestant ascendancy and of the city of Belfast that they had built. By sheer thrift, industry and reliability they had developed a city and a prosperity in the North which were the envy of the South. They had benefited from the Industrial Revolution in England while the South had hardly experienced it. Linen had succeeded cotton by 1830, and shipbuilding reached its height with the building of the ill-fated *Titanic* in 1911. Engineering, rope-making, flour-milling, tobacco, whiskey, chemicals, soap and glass were subsidiary industries. It was the Ulster people's belief that their union with Britain would not only strengthen these commercial interests but develop them. But in 1912, actors on the English and Southern Irish stage believed otherwise.

The Prime Minister, Herbert Asquith, although cautious in his political tactics, did not seem aware of how serious the opposition in Ulster was; or, if he was aware of it, he apparently thought of it merely as a bluff. Further, he did not consider the Bill very drastic in its effects on the relations between the two countries: although it set up an Irish parliament for the country, the absolute supremacy of the Westminister parliament over Dublin was affirmed in all matters. The Dublin parliament would control domestic matters, but would have no jurisdiction over taxation, the armed services or international treaties. The leader of the Irish Nationalist Party, John Redmond, seemed quite satisfied with these limitations, and acted in a gentlemanly way throughout. But it was apparent that he and his party were 'already growing dangerously out of touch with political feeling in Ireland'.[35] Forces of revolution were gathering there that would surface in 1916, and demonstrate that the Fenians and the Irish Republican Brotherhood were no longer prepared to wait for the politicians. The same warlike spirit was moving through Ulster before the debate on the Bill got under way. A vast crowd, estimated at around 100,000, marched through Belfast to hear the leader of the British Conservative Party, Andrew Bonar Law, pledge the help and support of his party for the Ulster resistance. But despite this support and the drilling of men throughout the province, the Bill reached its third reading, and this time the Lords could not impose a veto.

However, two events occurred in 1912 which reflected the differences between North and South. In Dublin there was great rejoicing over the passing of the Bill, with parades, bonfires and the singing of '*A Nation Once Again*', but in Belfast a resistance document called a 'Solemn League and Covenant' was signed.[36] The idea of a Covenant* reflects the plantation of Ulster by mainly Scotch people only a few years after the old Scotch Covenant of 1580. Inspired by this, a completely original Covenant was drafted,[37] reading as follows:

Being convinced in our consciences that Home Rule would be disastrous to the material well-being of Ulster as well as of the whole of Ireland, subversive of our civil and religious freedom, destructive of our citizenship, and perilous to the unity of the empire, we whose names are under written, men of Ulster, loyal subjects of His Gracious Majesty King George V, humbly relying on the God whom our fathers in days of stress and trial confidently trusted, do hereby pledge ourselves in solemn covenant throughout this our time of threatened calamity to stand by one another in defending for ourselves and our children our cherished position of equal citizenship in the United Kingdom, and in using all means which may be found necessary to defeat the present conspiracy to set up a Home Rule parliament in Ireland. And in the event of such a parliament being forced upon us we further solemnly and mutually pledge ourselves to refuse to recognise its authority. In sure confidence that God will defend the right, we hereto subscribe our names. And further, we individually declare that we have not already signed this covenant. God save the King.[38]

In the days that followed, demonstrations and parades were held all over Ulster leading up to Covenant Day, 28 September 1912. On this day,

---

* The reader may wish to know the basic details of the forerunners of the 1912 Covenant. The first was a contract between King James of Scotland and his subjects. From 1560 there had been conflict between the Crown and Kirk in Scotland; it was the power of the monarchy versus the power of the Church and people, who argued that having chosen the King they expected him to meet his obligations. So James signed in order to keep their loyalty and thus support the King's Confession of 1580.

In 1642 the English parliament, in the course of its quarrel with Charles I, sought Scottish assistance, and this led to its signing the 'Solemn League and Covenant' with the Scottish Convention of Estates and the General Assembly of the Church of Scotland, to promote the reformation of religion in England, while preserving the King's person and authority.

Ulster's Solemn League and Covenant reflects these ideas of Covenant, with the difference that support is for the Crown but not for any policy of a parliament that would force Home Rule upon them. This is discussed later in connection with the key concept of 'loyalty'.

with the sun shining on the proceedings, religious services were held in the morning and a vast crowd of people, complete with bands, sashes and banners, assembled in the centre of Belfast before the City Hall. Under the gaze of Queen Victoria's statue, Carson, Craig and various other dignitaries entered and signed the Covenant. Similar assemblies were held all over the country, and the final total of the people who followed their leaders in thus signing was 471,414. In Dublin, the Covenant was signed by 2,000 who had protested their opposition to Home Rule.[39] The next day Carson, after a tearful farewell to the people of Ulster, was greeted in Liverpool by a crowd of 150,000 at 7.30 a.m. on a Sunday morning.[40]

Words now gave way to action as Ulster mobilised 100,000 men, and arms were smuggled in from abroad. The commander was Sir George Richardson, an English general recently retired from the Indian Army. Further, the Liberal nerve really began to give way as General Gough and other British officers stationed at the Curragh camp in Dublin said that they would resign rather than move against Ulster. Asquith hovered on the brink of the Irish graveyard, as the King sent for him and suggested that a general election should be held before Home Rule was passed. This, together with the thought that Carson would set up a Provisional Government, 'mobilise the volunteers, take over the functions of the police and create a situation which would compel the intervention of troops',[41] compelled Asquith to seek a compromise. Winston Churchill, having experienced a 'hot' reception in Ulster because of his support for Home Rule, recommended that the province be excluded from Home Rule. This was eagerly seized upon by Carson.

In the House of Commons debate on 11 February 1914, Asquith announced that the government intended to bring forward proposals for dealing with the Ulster problem, and Carson appealed to the House in a dramatic speech which underlined that Ulster was fighting for the great principle of remaining under a government with which it was content as opposed to one which it loathed and detested. He pointed to the problem of the Southern Unionists and vowed that he would go on to the end with the Ulster resistance, which he argued was morally justifiable: 'Believe me, whatever way you settle the Irish question, there are only two ways to deal with Ulster. It is for statesmen to say which is the best and right one. She is not part of the community which can be bought. She will not allow herself to be sold. You must therefore coerce her if you go on — or you must, in the long run, by showing that good government can come under the Home Rule bill, try and win her over to the case of the rest of Ireland.'[42]

A world event now intervened that thrust the Home Rule Bill into the background: the Great War of 1914–18. The issue was officially suspended for as long as the war continued in the interests of national unity, and in May 1915 Carson joined the Asquith cabinet. But impatient revolutionaries in the South could not wait, and the Irish Republican Brotherhood, having brought into being the Irish Volunteers, staged the Dublin rising of 1916. This came to many as a surprise since many Southern Irishmen had volunteered to fight in the Irish regiments of the British army for the British cause against Germany. However, the fact was that in the South there were elements who agreed with Ulster on one thing at least: that Home Rule was a sell-out. The reasons were different, of course, and these appeared somewhat confused; but a clear one was that while England was at a disadvantage, the time was ripe to make a bid for complete freedom from the English yoke. This is not the place to go into detail concerning the rebellion, but when it was put down, Redmond and the Home Rule Party condemned the severity of the British action in putting it down and the executions that followed. The sympathy of the Irish went out to the defeated, and a political movement known as Sinn Fein (meaning 'Ourselves Alone') developed under the leadership of Eamon De Valera, one of the leaders of the 1916 rising. It stood for an independent sovereign republic, and in the general election of 1918 it gained the victory in Ireland. At this time, a force developed from the Irish Volunteers, the Citizens Army and the Irish Republican Brotherhood that is at the heart of Ulster's troubles today: the Irish Republican Army (I.R.A.). Its activity led to bitter conflict in Ireland. However, David Lloyd George, who had succeeded Asquith as Prime Minister in 1916, wanted to play the situation down, and said with somewhat excessive confidence, 'We have murder by the throat.'[43]

A truce was signed on 9 July 1921 and political manoeuvres began between Sinn Fein and the British government. This led to the Anglo-Irish treaty of 6 December and the creation of the Irish Free State; but this did not satisfy the I.R.A. who wanted a Republic. Ulster was included in the Treaty but given the choice of opting out, which it did as quickly as it could. Thus James Craig became the first Prime Minister of the Ulster parliament (Stormont) set up to govern the six counties of Antrim, Armagh, Derry, Down, Fermanagh and Tyrone. Republicans were enraged by this settlement, not only because of partition, but because the members of the Free State parliament had to take an oath of allegiance to the King. The inevitable result was civil war in the South (June 1922) between those who accepted the Treaty for the time being and those, like De Valera, who did not. Trouble also broke out in Ulster because of fear that the Boundary Commission might undermine its new political entity.[44] The I.R.A. extended its operations to Ulster in order, as it said, to protect the Catholics — and this brought a new force into the field against them: The Ulster Special Constabulary. This consisted of three grades of police: full-time 'A Specials', part-time 'B Specials' and the 'C Specials' who had no regular duties. Membership was usually Protestant, and was recruited from the Ulster Volunteer Force which had been formed to resist Home Rule.

The South itself was in a pitiable situation with two wings of the I.R.A. fighting one another and the Irish people in the middle. The Treaty supporters finally won, but the Minister for Home Affairs in the Irish parliament (the Dail), Kevin Higgins (assassinated on 10 July 1927), must have been reflecting on Carson's words when he said:

'We had an opportunity of building up a worthwhile state that would attract and in time assimilate those elements [Ulster]. . . . We preferred to burn our own houses, blow up our own bridges, rob our own banks, saddle ourselves with millions of debt for the maintainance of an army. . . . Generally we preferred to practise upon ourselves worse indignities than the British had practiced on us since Cromwell . . . and now we wonder why the Orangemen are not hopping like so many fleas across the border in their anxiety to come within our fold and jurisdiction. . . .'[45]

De Valera, however, reorganised his Sinn Fein party and called it Fianna Fail ('Warriors of Ireland'). He came to power as Prime Minister in 1932 and eventually had to declare the I.R.A. an illegal organisation in 1936. A new Constitution in 1937 virtually made Ireland a Republic in all but name, and Britain handed over to her the military and naval rights to the Irish ports — an action which was to prove costly in the Second World War. Winston Churchill, in a broadcast speech in May 1945, praised Northern Ireland for its loyalty and friendship during the war that had just ended, and said that without it Britain might have had to occupy the Republic of Ireland.[46]

This loyalty to Britain — though put under severe test, as we have seen — remains the dominant characteristic of the Ulster Protestant. How it has worked in Ulster and how the post-1969 troubles arose we will return to in Chapter 4. We now need to examine another dominant trait which has influenced both the thinking and the behaviour of Ulster people since the days of the Plantation: allegiance to the Protestant faith.

REFERENCES

1. J.C. Beckett, *A Short History of Ireland*, 3rd edn, London: Hutchinson, 1966, p. 32.
2. E. Curtis, *A History of Ireland*, 6th edn, London: Methuen, 1950, p. 205.
3. Beckett, op. cit., p. 60.
4. Ibid., p. 66.
5. Curtis, op. cit., p. 229. On the whole matter, see E. Curtis and R.B. McDowell, *Irish Historical Documents*, 1172–1922, London: Methuen, 1943, pp. 128ff.
6. Curtis, op. cit., p. 232.
7. Robert Kee, *Ireland: A History*, London: Weidenfeld and Nicolson, 198, p. 41.
8. R. Bagwell, *Ireland under the Tudors*, 3 vols, Longmans, Green, 1885–90, vol. 2, p. 80.
9. Kee, op. cit., p. 44.
10. Beckett, op. cit., p. 79.
11. Ibid., p. 81.
12. Ibid., p. 90; cf. Kee, op. cit., p. 48.
13. Ibid., p. 93; cf. E.M. Johnston, *Ireland in the Eighteenth Century*, Dublin: Gill and Macmillan, p. 1974.
14. Kee, op. cit., p. 49; cf. Curtis, op. cit., p. 271.
15. Kee, op. cit., p. 50.
16. M. MacCurtain, *Tudor and Stuart in Ireland*, Dublin: Gill and Macmillan, pp. 184–5.
17. A.T.Q. Stewart, *The Ulster Crisis*, London: Faber and Faber, 1967, p. 29.
18. Beckett, op. cit., p. 126.
19. Ibid., p. 129.
20. Ibid., p. 142.
21. Ibid., p. 145.
22. Ibid., p. 156.
23. Curtis, op. cit., p. 383.
24. Stewart, op. cit., p. 21.
25. Ibid., p. 25.
26. Kee, op. cit., p. 123.
27. T. Downing (ed.), *The Troubles*, Macdonald Futura, 1980, p. 56.
28. Liam de Paor, *Divided Ulster*, Harmondsworth: Pelican Books, 1970, p. 44.
29. Brian Faulkner, *Memoirs of a Statesman*, London: Weidenfeld and Nicolson, 1978, p. 44.
30. E. Gallagher and S. Worrall, *Christians in Ulster, 1968–1980*, Oxford University Press, 1982, p. 195.
31. Ibid., pp. 197–8.
32. Curtis, op. cit., p. 386.
33. Stewart, op. cit., p. 41.
34. Ibid., p. 42.
35. Ibid., p. 36.
36. Ibid., p. 64.
37. Ibid., p. 62.
38. E. Curtis and R.B. McDowell, *Irish Historical Documents*, p. 304.
39. Stewart, op. cit., p. 65.
40. Ibid., p. 66.
41. Ibid., p. 80.

42. Curtis and McDowell, op. cit., p. 306.
43. Kee, op. cit., p. 188.
44. Ibid., p. 195.
45. Ibid., p. 205.
46. Ibid., p. 220.

3

THE RELIGIOUS FACTOR

A.T.Q. Stewart says that in Ulster 'the difference in religion was of incalculable importance', and certainly not only Ulster but the whole of Ireland has been influenced in every sphere of its life by the Protestant or the Catholic faith.

But thousands of years before the birth of Christ, tombs and monuments to the dead were being raised with their entrances facing the rising sun — they are to be seen today on archaeological sites — and thus pointing to the sun worship of the inhabitants in those times. With the arrival of the Gaels from Gaul about the first century BC, druidism became prominent, but gradually Christianity came to be known, probably brought by traders operating between Ireland and Roman Britain. Thus there were Christians in the country before the arrival of St Patrick in AD 432, and they were sufficiently numerous by 431 'to justify the appointment of a bishop for them by Rome in that year'.[1]

Scholars differ regarding the dates of both his arrival and his death, but there is little doubt about the remarkable work of evangelism, ecclesiastical order, monasticism, culture and language that he accomplished. From his work was to emerge the great missionary outreach of the Irish Church to the mainland, where Christianity was being destroyed by the Anglo-Saxon invaders. St Columba of Derry founded the monastery of Iona in 563 and from there reached out to southern Scotland and northern England. St Columbanus travelled from Bangor to Burgundy and Italy, and St Kilian, St Fiachra, St Fursa and St Lininius evangelised other parts of Europe. 'Wherever they went these saints founded monasteries; Lindisfarne, St Gall, Bobbio, are perhaps the most famous links in a chain which stretched from the British Isles to Italy.'[2] This desire to evangelise, which was so evident in the earliest beginnings of Christianity in Ireland, is taken up again in the Protestant faith, and is a central aspect not only of the various sects but of the mainline Churches in Ulster today.

Patrick's mission centred itself finally in the north-east of Ulster, and after he had worked there for twelve years, a local prince presented him with a site for a church at Armagh, which was destined to be the metropolis of Irish Christianity. According to Curtis, we cannot doubt that Patrick was a typical western Christian of his age, holding to the Latin

Eucharist, the invocation of saints, the sacraments and the doctrine of the Catholic faith as held generally in his time, and that he must have regarded the Bishop of Rome as the final authority in spiritual matters.[3] This Catholic church was strong in education and culture: Irish monasteries flourished and produced the *Book of Durrow* (a seventh-century transcription of the Gospels), the Ardagh chalice of the early eighth century and the *Book of Kells* (also Gospels). It also sent abroad scholars such as John Scotus, who became chief professor at the palace school of the Emperor Charles the Bald at Laon, and was not only the greatest intellect given by Ireland to Europe at that time but also one of the most brilliant scholars produced by the renaissance of the age of Charlemagne.[4] Thus the Church in Ireland, with its centre in Ulster, exercised a civilising influence. Patrick, says Curtis, 'turned the Irish from a race of cruel conquerors, whose galleys were dreaded on all the coasts of Britain and Gaul, into a race whose enthusiasm was for missionary labour, Latin learning, and the contemplative life.'[5]

Religion, now unified to some extent, might have been an inspiration and an impetus towards a political unity, but this did not happen, and the country was an easy prey for the invaders who followed: the Norsemen (Danes, they were called in Ireland), Vikings and Normans. The Norsemen did great harm to the monasteries, plundering, robbing and destroying, and only when Brian Boru defeated them at Clontarf on the outskirts of Dublin did the Church have the opportunity to recover. The Norsemen eventually became Christian, but their bishops were subject to Canterbury and not to Armagh, and this caused much dissension and disunity in the years that followed. However, the Norse invasion and settlement showed Irish churchmen that they were diverging from the rest of Western Christendom, and by the middle of the twelfth century this led to a better organisation of the Church. Four archbishops were consecrated — at Armagh, Dublin, Cashel and Tuam — with each receiving his pallium from the Pope. Under the reign of Henry II, other reforms were initiated in order to bring the Irish Church into line with the English.[6]

Armagh was the centre of the Irish Church and Canterbury of the English. Papal authority over the world Church had generally favoured the supremacy of Canterbury over Armagh, and this at times caused friction with the Irish Church. Thus at the time of the Reformation under Henry VIII, the lack of love felt by the Irish Church for the papal authority encouraged it to accept the headship of the King without much difficulty.[7] Hence the failure of the Jesuit missionaries, who arrived in Ulster in 1542 with letters from the Pope, and had to make a speedy return to Scotland. Still, in matters of worship, the Catholic Church in Ireland did not completely accept the *Book of Common Prayer* of 1549, and it was only with Elizabeth that both the Act of Supremacy and the Act of Uniformity were passed by the Dublin parliament in 1560. However, little attention was paid to these, and there was no Cranmer to continue the Reformation process as in England. But the attempt to impose them stimulated Catholicism, and the Counter-Reformation was able to lay 'the foundation of that devotion to the Roman Catholic faith which has long been characteristic of the bulk of the population of Ireland'.[8] The papacy became popular, and nationalism was associated with it.

Because Elizabeth established the Anglican Church in Ireland, her work is important; from that time a Protestant population grew up which was reinforced by the colonists, especially the Ulster Plantation.[9] Ulster thus became a province almost entirely Protestant as regards the landowners and mainly so as regards the population, with a special provision being made for the established Church.[10] Thus in the seventeenth century Anglicans, Presbyterians (Scots) and Catholics (native Irish) were living side by side. The Anglo-Irish were the governing class, with large estates and a devotion to the Anglican Church. J.C. Beckett says that their striking characteristics were 'arrogance and ambivalence'.[11] Their favourite sport was riding to hounds, and the locals irreverently referred to them as 'the horse Protestants'. The link between the 'Big House' and the Church was strong, with the local gentry prominent in administration and patronage. Trinity College in Dublin was the bastion of their culture, where their sons and the sons of the clergy were educated.

In Church administration there was a difference between Anglicanism and Presbyterianism, which was to divide them socially in terms not only of class but of religion. Presbyterians are Calvinists, who hold that man is depraved but that a certain number of people have been elected by God to eternal life. This means that Christ only died for that number, and that he will save them by his irresistible grace and preserve them to the end. Anglicanism in its Evangelical form, as expressed in the *Thirty-Nine Articles of the Church of England*, has a similarity of doctrine with this Calvinism, as expressed in the Presbyterian standard, the *Westminster Confession of Faith*.

It is in the government of the Church that differences arise between the two denominations. Presbyterians believe that the laity have a vital part to play and that the management should be in the hands of representatives of the people. These are called presbyters or elders, and they are elected by each congregation and represent the people in the Church courts which are the Session, the Presbytery, the Synod and the General Assembly. The minister of the local congregation is also a teaching elder and presides at the meeting of the Session of the Church. He is called to be minister by the votes of the entire congregation. Several different words are used in Scripture for these representatives of the Church, but the Presbyterian believes that they all indicate the same office. Here controversy arises with Anglicanism, for the Anglicans interpret one of these words, *episcopos*, as meaning bishop, whereas the Presbyterians, translating it literally as 'overseer', say that it means the same as elder, pastor or minister. No distinction, they say, is to be made between the duties of a bishop and those of the ordinary minister or pastor.

Even those who are elected to be moderators of the various Church courts are considered merely as *primus inter pares* (first among equals). But with the Anglicans or Catholics, authority resides in the bishop, and the people are not represented as in the Presbyterian system. Presbyterians rest their case on what happened in the early Church when a council was held to make decisions (*Acts* 15). The decisions concerning the future of the Church were taken by elders representing the various local Churches. Thus Presbyterians deny the right of a bishop to have the right of ordination of clergy, as if some virtue were transmitted through the 'apostolic succession' by physical contact. From this religious belief stems an important trait: democracy. This led the Presbyterian to demand religious, political and social equality for all, and if these could not be achieved by constitutional means, then it was necessary to engage in revolution.

In this Scottish Presbyterianism there was also a Puritanical strain which showed itself in church architecture, the conduct of worship, disciplined attendance, the keeping of the Sabbath, dress and behaviour. The mark of a Presbyterian church building was its 'barn-like' shape with tall box-pews and central high pulpit. No pictures, crosses or ecclesiastical ornamentation of any kind were allowed; and the communion table was placed at the side, to show that the sacrament took second place after the preaching of the word. In many churches up to the end of the nineteenth century the use of instrumental music was forbidden, and only Psalms were sung. Organs were introduced towards the end of the century, but some churches still refused to have them. The Sabbath was strictly observed; meals were prepared the day before, and all restaurants and places of entertainment were closed. Even in the late twentieth century visitors from England complained about the difficulty of finding an eating place open in Belfast and the boredom resulting from the lack of any kind of entertainment. There has been controversy in relatively recent times over the closing of public parks on the Sabbath, with newspapers saying that such austerity deprived children of the use of harmless games and enjoyment.

The adults, of course, derived their pleasure from the long and weighty sermons which thundered from the pulpits, and they would discuss and debate the content when they returned home. The local papers devoted pages both to advertising church services and to reporting them. Indeed, as F.S.L. Lyons points out, 'The sermon was thus a major, perhaps the major, cultural experience shared by the whole community, something to be "tasted" and discussed throughout the following week. Since devout households did not admit much profane literature, abominated cards and billiards, and looked askance at the theatre and later the cinema, the minister's only rivals were politicians' speeches, generally cast in a similar mould; the more solid newspapers, particularly the *Belfast Telegraph* and the missionary and other magazines turned out in great profusion by the Presbyterian Church itself.'[12] Sobriety of dress and behaviour, and temperance, were stressed right at the beginning, and have continued to this day. In England it is taken for granted that the Irish are prone to drunkenness, and this tendency has indeed caused trouble wherever they have settled on the mainland. The English are therefore very surprised to find Ulster people frowning on their own temperate drinking, and refusing to touch any alcohol at all. They are unaware that this strict Presbyterianism had even refused the use of fermented wine in the Communion services of the Church.[13]

We will consider later this Puritan ethic in relation to the industrialisation and prosperity of the North, but now we have to examine the uneasy tension and virtual hatred that developed between the two strands of Christianity — the Protestant and the Catholic. The Protestant ascendancy that emerged in Ulster was that of the Anglicans; there was discrimination against the Presbyterians and Catholics. The Catholics had been deprived of their land as a result of the Plantation and their rebellion in 1641 against the settlers; and the Presbyterians suffered in various ways. Only Anglicans were appointed as Justices of the Peace, and Presbyterian marriages were declared invalid. Further, it was decreed that the sacrament must be taken according to the Anglican rite. But the 1641 rebellion united the Protestants — Anglicans together with Presbyterians —, since they were massacred without distinction.

This implanted in the Presbyterians a fear of the Catholics and a resolution to unite with the Anglicans against their common foe whenever such emergencies arose. In turn, the awful revenge that Cromwell exacted for the massacre of the Protestants produced a hatred in the Catholics. Thus the demarcation lines in Ulster were strongly drawn in the years following the settlement. Cromwell left such a deep mark on the Catholics that to this day they still speak of 'the curse of Cromwell', but he also strongly influenced Presbyterianism. It was not only that he confirmed their Puritanism, but the republican idea that he represented appealed to their deeply ingrained democratic instincts, and they do not find it inconsistent today with an ideological loyalty to the British Crown. They may have agreed with his statement, 'I meddle not with any man's conscience but as for the liberty to exercise the mass, I must tell you that where the Parliament of England has power, that will not be allowed';[14] but they also fully accepted the Protestant civil liberty, equality and democracy that he proclaimed. In the face of continued Anglican persecution, some of them were willing to go further and extend this to liberty and equality for all — even to the Catholics!

There was to be a division here, of course, between those Presbyterians who were liberal enough to embrace the cause of individual rights, whatever a person's religion might be, and those who saw everything in terms of religion. The latter tended to fanaticism and fully followed Cromwell's ideas. Their fanatical zeal and violence find an echo today in the preaching of some clergy in Northern Ireland, denouncing what they call heresy. The Roman 'harlot' must be destroyed and rooted out of the province, and no Roman representative will be received (Pope John Paul, it will be remembered, wisely chose not to come to Ulster when he visited Ireland in 1979). The events of the seige of Derry and the victory over James II at the battle of the Boyne seem to confirm to the Presbyterians that their religion is true — and that God must be a Protestant. It did not occur to them then, and most are blissfully unaware now, that William had actually been fighting on the side of the Pope against France, and been equipped with arms by him under the Treaty of Augsburg.

Under William and Mary, William III alone and then Anne (1691–1714), the parliaments of both England and Ireland were called upon to take an oath of allegiance to the Crown and make a declaration against the mass, transubstantiation and other Roman doctrines and a denial of the supremacy of the Pope.[15] The time of the Protestant ascendancy in Ireland had begun and was to last for the next century and a half. The

Presbyterians rejoiced in this, but such enjoyment was not to last for long.

It is true that the reign of William is particularly sweet to Presbyterians since their ministers received the *regium donum*, a monetary grant from the King which was to be distributed among them. However, the Anglicans, jealous of the numbers and growing prosperity of the Presbyterians, renewed their objections to Presbyterianism. It was decreed that the Presbyterian minister was not an ordained clergyman according to the law unless he had been ordained by a bishop, and that marriages performed by him were therefore not valid. Presbyterians had to pay tithes to the Anglican clergy, and an Act of 1704 required all public officeholders under the Crown to qualify by taking the sacrament according to the rite of the established Church. This in effect excluded Protestant dissenters from all public office whether of the state or under local corporations. Before this, the Presbyterians had had the vote and returned some Members of Parliament, but now their representatives were excluded, and to add to their sorrows the *regium donum* was withdrawn in 1710; increases in rents added fuel to the fire. Presbyterians emigrated to the American colonies in the hope of finding political and religious equality. Even the easing of the situation by the restoration of the *regium donum* in 1718 and the Toleration Act of 1719 did not satisfy the dissenters, because the test clause for office still remained.[16] The Anglicans behaved in this way towards the Presbyterians not only because they wanted to retain their place as the governing class but also because they suspected the Presbyterians of republican tendencies and thus of disloyalty to the Crown.

Of course, the Catholics fared much worse. They had to endure exclusion from Parliament and from Trinity College Dublin, and they could not send their children overseas to be educated. They had to take the oath of allegiance if they wanted to practice law, they were excluded from office in corporations, they could not join the army, nor could they vote in elections. Further, they were denied the right to acquire Protestant land, and their bishops were banished. These penal laws lasted seventy years.[17] At the beginning of the eighteenth century, Catholics had to celebrate mass on altars in ruined churches and in the open air. Parish priests were allowed to officiate if they registered with the authorities, but friars were sent abroad. This placed the Church in a dilemma, for if there were no bishops or archbishops, how were candidates for the priesthood to be ordained? However, the religious laws were not rigidly enforced, and not all bishops were actually expelled, so the Church did not die out. As long as the Catholics showed loyalty to the Crown and kept the civil law, a blind eye could be turned to breaches of religious practice. But because many of the Catholic landowners, being penalised by the laws, left the country for Britain or the continent, the leadership of the peasantry fell to the priests. This was very significant for the future of the country, for with it nationalism and Catholicism in Ireland became entwined for the first time. As Beckett says, 'The great political power of the Catholic church in modern Ireland can be traced directly to the effectiveness of the eighteenth-century penal code.'[18]

Signs of the coming conflict were the growth of the peasant trade unions divided on sectarian lines: 'White-boys' (who wore white shirts) were drawn from the Catholics, while the 'Steel-boys' and 'Oak-boys' (who wore oak leaves in their hats) were Presbyterians. But what caused the explosion was the Society for United Irishmen, in which Presbyterians and Catholics united to promote parliamentary reform and the unification of both into one nation. This was a remarkable event when compared with the fear, distrust and hatred of the seventeenth century. In the light of today's hatred and violence between Catholic and Protestant in the North of Ireland, it appears more remarkable still. There are a number of explanations for this. First, both the Ulster Presbyterians and the Irish Catholics had suffered terribly under the penal laws. Secondly, there was the sense of injustice felt by the Presbyterians, who had fought for the Protestant faith and been rewarded by the penal code. Thirdly, there were the republican ideas stemming from Cromwell and, even more potent, the cry of liberty that resounded throughout Europe with the French Revolution. Thus the battle of the Boyne was allied to the fall of the Bastille, and both were celebrated in Belfast.[19]

The democratic ideas that we have seen as the bedrock of Presbyterian Church government reached a climax in this movement, which demanded equal rights for all. And the political and religious ideas of liberty and fraternity combined in 1791 to form the Society of United Irishmen. Religious labels were abandoned, and the Protestant founder, Wolfe Tone, attacked the Established Church as the bastion of the prevailing injustice of the time. Tone's own beliefs took the form of a sort of deism, stressing a rational approach to religion. His view of the dissenters of the North is significant:

The dissenters of the north, and more especially of the town of Belfast, are, from the genius of their religion and from the superior diffusion of political information among them, sincere and enlightened republicans. They had even been foremost in the pursuit of Parliamentary reform, and I have already mentioned the early wisdom of the town of Belfast in proposing the emancipation of the Catholics as far back as the year 1783. The French Revolution awakened all parties in the nation from the stupor in which they lay plunged . . . and the citizens of Belfast were first to raise their heads from the abyss, and to look the situation of their country steadily in the face.[20]

The agitation raised by the movement had some effect in leading to the Catholic Relief Act of 1793, which brought some help to the Catholics: it allowed them to vote in the counties and boroughs, to act as grand jurors, to take degrees in Dublin University, to hold minor offices, and to take commissions in the army below the rank of General.[21] But they had no seats in Parliament or offices in the government, for this still required them to receive the sacrament according to the Anglican rite and to subscribe to the anti-Roman declaration of 1692.

The movement of United Irishmen failed for a number of reasons. Extremists gained control in 1796, and attempted an insurrection, but the expected French help failed to materialise. The British army used ruthless methods to put down the rebellion in Ulster, and by 1797 the conspiracy in that part of Ireland was virtually broken (the main rebellion in Ireland took place the following year).[22] Another factor in its failure was that although thousands of Presbyterians had joined the movement, many had not done so because the Synod of Ulster had condemned it. Thus the Society divided Presbyterianism. Further, the rise of Orange societies in 1795 recreated the old sectarian divisions and, although these societies were originally composed of Anglicans, they began to make inroads into Presbyterianism. One of the declared Orange objectives was to 'maintain the laws and peace of the country and Protestant institutions'. But the United Irishmen movement had been fired by national feeling, radical democracy and social discontent. Some of these characteristics were to lead to a division among the Presbyterians in the nineteenth century between conservatives and those who rejected Calvinism in favour of a more liberal, moderate and humanistic approach.[23]

At the beginning of the nineteenth century the Act of Union took place; William Pitt the Younger, the Prime Minister, was convinced that the only way to deal with the revolutionary tendency in Ireland was to unify the countries under the British Crown.

The mainly Anglican Anglo-Irish had been caught between the radical democracy of the Presbyterians and the Catholic revival, and this showed them that the only way to keep the dissenters apart — a case of 'divide and rule' — was to foster fear of the Catholics in the minds of the Ulster Protestants. This became the policy of the Unionist Party in Northern Ireland and the Conservatives in Britain. Still, they and the Orange societies resisted the Union, being themselves afraid that they would thereby lose their ascendancy, and because of the promises made by Pitt to the Catholics: he had calmed their fears by bringing about a union of the English and Irish Churches to form the 'United Church of England and Ireland' and undertaking to maintain the ecclesiastical establishment. And the olive branch was held out to the Catholics too, with a state provision for the maintenance of their clergy and for episcopal elections. Further, Catholics were to be admitted to Parliament. This policy became known as 'Catholic emancipation', and in fact did not come to fulfilment till 1829. The Presbyterians reluctantly agreed to the Union in order to safeguard their trade with mainland Britain and the growing prosperity of their region. But their main reason for doing so appeared to be the revival of the old fear of the Catholics, with sectarian division showing itself in the North, and the rise of the new nationalism advocated by Daniel O'Connell.

O'Connell repudiated the Union, saying that he would prefer to have the penal laws; and, to the alarm of the Ulster Protestants, he identified his movement firmly with Catholicism. Under his guidance the Catholic Association, founded in 1823, received new impetus, and the parish priest assumed a key role by collecting money for the cause from his parishioners. The whole of the peasantry were aroused in this movement for Catholic emancipation, which had been promised by Pitt but had not materialised. This alliance with Catholicism gave the anti-Union cause great power, but it alienated the last remnants of Presbyterian nationalism and drove them into the Anglican camp.

Encouraged by an increase in the *regium donum* to their ministers, the Presbyterians saw the Reverend Henry Cooke, Moderator of the Ulster Synod, as their champion against O'Connell. He was 'an orator not altogether unworthy of comparison with O'Connell himself, and in power of invective perhaps even his equal. Under Cooke's guidance the Presbyterians definitely ranged themselves beside the established Church in defence of the union.'[24] Still, democracy and a demand for religious equality remained strong in the Ulster Protestant character.[25] With the passing of the Emancipation Bill in 1829 and the dissenters benefiting at the same time from the removal of the sacramental Test, the Orange Order was discouraged and broke up in 1837 (it revived in 1845). O'Connell had done much to move towards his goal of an independent

Ireland, but it was left to others to achieve it as events moved towards Home Rule.

Before considering the influence and impact of religion on Home Rule, we need to consider two other events, the Non-Subscribing controversy and the Evangelical Awakening or Revival, which show, on the one hand, a rational element in the Ulster character and, on the other, an emotional one. Both events have a religious context. Presbyterians believe in faith and grace, but also excel in rational dispute and argument over the content of their faith. Since the Church system is essentially democratic, such debates caused meetings to carry on into the small hours of the morning. They would, typically, be centred on such abstract matters as sin and grace, 'election', the person of Christ, and the Trinity. The Presbyterian did not heed the warning, 'If you can lose your soul by denying the Trinity, you can lose your wits trying to understand it.' The inevitable result was division. In the eighteenth century there was schism between those who favoured subscription to the *Westminster Confession of Faith* of 1643 and those — called Non-Subscribing Presbyterians — who opposed it. Then there was a further split caused by those who thought the Church system too centralised; these were known as Seceders.

The Non-Subscribing dispute, which continued into the nineteenth century, centred around the personal duel between two leading divines: Henry Cooke (his opponents called him the 'Presbyterian Pope') and Henry Montgomery. It was 'a battle between liberalism and conservatism and the latter, in the person of Henry Cooke, triumphed, though at the cost of further secessions.'[26] Among the reasons put forward for these secessions is the allegation that it was personal rivalry generated by the emergence of two outstanding orators in the Ulster Synod. Each recognised the other's greatness. Cooke said that Montgomery 'had the greatest command of the English language of any man living'. Montgomery was as generous about Cooke: 'His dexterity as a debater I have never seen surpassed, whether in defending his own weak points or attacking those of his adversary — his eloquence during our synodical debates was frequently commanding, and the skill with which he played on all the chords of the popular heart was perfect.'[27]

When they met in dispute it was an encounter of ecclesiastical gladiators. Cooke excelled in extempore speech, reasoned argument and invective, while Montgomery was more graceful in speech with great powers of persuasion and an ability to 'turn a light-hearted audience to tears, and a tearful one back to smiles'.[28] In debate Cooke outstripped

Montgomery, and with his sparkling wit and repartee he was frequently able to crush his opponent. The excitement caused by these debates was so great that the newspapers sometimes contained nothing else worthy of note. In the crowded Synod meetings, wooden planks were placed from pew to pew across the aisles, and dignified ministers were glad of a seat upon them.[29] The battle with Montgomery was the second controversy concerning subscription to the *Westminster Confession of Faith*, and with the victory of Cooke in 1835, subscription to the *Confession* was made binding on all ministers, licentiates and elders in the Synod. The Non-Subscribing Presbyterians left the Church, and entered eventually into communion with the Unitarian and Free Christian Churches of Great Britain. Apart from the personal rivalry of these two men and the difference in theological opinion, another reason has been put forward for the secession. Cooke was a Tory and an opponent of 'Catholic emancipation', whereas Montgomery was a Liberal and ardently supported it.[30]

We have noted that there were many Presbyterians in the Society of United Irishmen in the eighteenth century who repudiated British rule in Ireland, and that to achieve this end they united with the Catholics. The Non-Subscribers asserted in the nineteenth-century conflict that Cooke was determined to destroy this political radicalism and encourage loyalism and the cause of unionism. In fairness to Cooke, it must be admitted that he did not oppose 'limited emancipation' for the Catholics, but he used the Orange support for loyalism to the Crown to gain his theological victory. Montgomery, who was an ardent supporter of Catholic claims, said of Cooke: 'Thus uniting Evangelicalism with Orangeism and the countenance of the aristocracy with the applause of the multitude, in a few months . . . he had acquired extraordinary popularity and influence.'[31] Montgomery himself admitted that he had his best friends among those who had been involved in the cause of the United Irishmen, and he could almost certainly never have subscribed to the *Westminster Confession of Faith*, not only because of the Trinity (he was an Arian), but because it named the Pope as the anti-Christ.

The whole debate demonstrates how politics and religion were interwoven in Ulster. Besides the determining factor of religion, social and political forces had been at work, or had been put to work.[32] Mainline Presbyterianism in Ulster thus became Evangelical and conservative, although many liberals remained in the Synod and today the General Assembly is about equally divided, as the voting for Professors shows. But the Non-Subscribers had displayed a remarkable rationality and willingness to speculate in theology, and included some of the best-educated people in the Province.

When the dust had settled on the Non-Subscribing controversy, the earlier Seceders, convinced of the orthodoxy of the Synod of Ulster, were reunited with it to form the General Assembly of the Presbyterian Church in Ireland. Grace and faith had triumphed over rationality, and the ground was prepared for an event which showed the emotional aspect of the Ulster Protestant: the 'Great Revival' of 1859. The Non-Subscribing controversies were a reaction against the severity of Calvinism, and this same Calvinism was opposed by the emotion of the Revival. Ulster shared this revival with similar outbreaks in Britain and North America, where reports were circulated of mass conversions and of people suffering seizures. *The Times* was in opposition to the movement, but noted that it was unusual for it to occur among Ulstermen, who were cool, practical, money-making, fond of disputation, hard-headed and logical.[33] All denominations were involved, although the Presbyterians played the leading role. In terms of ethical behaviour, missionary work and growth in the Churches, the revival was beneficial and hardly deserved to be described (in the words of hostile critics) as the 'year of delusion'. The Non-Subscribers or Unitarians were generally antagonistic, and urged their ministers to impede the movement, and the reactions of the Catholics varied from mere denunciation to actual violence: 'Roman Catholic mobs attacked Evangelical ministers and people on the streets in many places and even besieged them in their homes.'[34] The priests in particular were opposed because a number of their flock were converted to Protestantism:

The revival fostered the Evangelical spirit of all denominations and led to the founding of the Keswick Convention Movement for the Deepening of the Spiritual Life, which has since exercised an emotional and ethical influence, in Britain and in Northern Ireland. Great crowds of Evangelical Protestants gather at Portstewart in Co. Londonderry every year for the week of the Convention, and reveal a unity that easily transcends the denominational lines of Anglican, Presbyterian and so on. Moody and Sankey extended the revival with their work of evangelism in 1874, when many conversions were recorded, and indeed Ulster with its highest Church attendance in the United Kingdom became the happy hunting-ground for American evangelists. However, the roots of sectarian division sank deeper during the nineteenth century over the question of education. Here religion again figured as the dominant dividing factor. A national system of education was established in 1831 with government grants for primary schools, and religious instruction was to be given to children at times when their clergy could attend. However, in 1840 Presbyterians refused to admit clergy of other denominations into their schools, and thus children of other denominations received instruction from Presbyterian ministers. The result was the withdrawal of children who were not Presbyterians and, consequently, a proliferation of small primary schools throughout the country.[35] The Catholic Church itself remained outside the state system, believing that the control of the religious education of its children was essential to survival.[36] Thus, from the beginning of their education in Ulster, children are separated socially and culturally from the children of other religions (to the average Protestant in Ulster, Catholicism means another religion, not merely another denomination of the same religion), and it is only in later years, if they happen to go on to higher education, that they can meet. But the history of the conflict would indicate that by this stage it is too late.

We must now consider the religious factor in the controversy over the Home Rule Bills. Gladstone, we have seen, was partial to Home Rule for Ireland, and his first step in 1869 was to disestablish and disendow the Irish Church. This, removing the privileged position of Anglicanism as the state religion and marking the beginning of the end for Protestant ascendancy, came as a shock to the Anglo-Irish. In the eighteenth century these Anglicans had displayed a peculiar nationalism of their own, which went far in the Irish direction, but always with loyalty to the Crown and allegiance to the British connection. Parnell was one of them, and in his support for Home Rule he had little sympathy for traditional Irish nationalism and the revival of Ireland as a Gaelic nation.[37] They did agreed with Ulster in its belief in a union with Britain, but were virtually free from religious prejudice and did not take the Calvinism of the North very seriously.[38] The Catholics and the Presbyterians rejoiced in this overthrow of ecclesiastical dominance which had cost them so much over the years, but of course they were divided over Home Rule.

The anti-Home Rule slogan of Protestant dissenters — 'Home Rule is Rome rule' — has survived to this day. They see the South of Ireland as priest-ridden, controlled in some way by the Vatican, and ready at every opportunity to take away their civil and religious liberties. How much truth is there in this slogan? We cannot answer this question fully here, and it recurs in the next chapter as we consider the historical and religious factors from the founding of the Stormont parliament. But in the context of the late nineteenth and early twentieth century, it is worth seeking a preliminary answer. Curtis maintains, on the contrary, that 'the Irish take their politics from Ireland and their religion from Rome.' The freedom of the old Irish Catholic Church from Rome in the earliest centuries resulted partly from geographical isolation but also partly from inclination. Curtis himself gives two illustrations of the rejection of papal control in the nineteenth century. Parnell urged the peasants to keep a firm grip on their homesteads, and declared that it was right to boycott those who took farms from which the original tenants had been evicted. Most of the Catholic bishops were opposed to this policy, and when the Pope in 1882 supported them and tried to interfere with the rights of property and with the law of contract, the state ruled him out of order. Again in 1882, when a national subscription was started for Parnell, the Pope sent a letter to the Irish bishops condemning it and forbidding faithful Catholics to subscribe. But most of the people refused to obey, and some £40,000 was raised.[39] Against Curtis' view we have the contention that it was the power of the Catholic Church that caused the downfall of Parnell in the case of Mrs O'Shea; that it is the Catholic Church that maintains the separation of education; and that in 1908 it declared marriages between Roman Catholics and Protestants invalid according to the *Ne Temere* decree promulgated by the Council of Trent in 1564 (a later relaxation of the decree being withdrawn). So we can probably say with some justice that although over the years the papal power has greatly diminished in political and social life, the binding together of nationalism and Catholicism that was so well developed by O'Connell was too recent in the mind of Ulster Protestants to allow them to withdraw their slogan about 'Rome Rule' when the Home Rule issue came to the forefront of the political arena.

And of course religion was used in the service of politics. When we consider all the rebellions, insurrections and wars that have marked the relation between England and Ireland, England's reluctance to grant Ireland freedom is astonishing. The reasons lay in the strategic position of Ireland as a backdoor for an enemy to attack England, and in the English nationalism which regarded Ireland as valuable both as a market and a source for its food supply.[40] Hence the policy of the Conservative Party during the Home Rule controversy of 'playing the Orange card' and encouraging the Ulster Protestants to unite against the Catholics. In short, politics hardened the religious sectarian division.

Again religion strengthened politics when the entire ceremony of signing the Covenant in 1912 was blessed by religion. The Covenant itself was submitted to the Protestant Churches for approval, and an important change was made regarding the signatories at the suggestion of the Presbyterians. This was that the obligation on the signatories should be confined to the present crisis, since no one could foresee what circumstances might arise in the future.[41] On the day of the Covenant, the congregations in hundreds of churches sang, as in a time of national crisis, 'O God, our Help in Ages Past', and the representatives of the Protestant Churches were foremost in signing it.[42] No doubt there were religious fanatics among that vast crowd, but many were moderate folk praying that there would be no violence and merely hoping that the link with Britain would be maintained. The Ulster people, as we have noted, are cool and quite logical, but even moderates can be aroused when religion and patriotism are at stake so that they will fight for what they believe to be right. This liberalism, moderation and rationality were to be found among the Presbyterians in the Non-Subscribing debates in the Synod of Ulster, and although the conservatives, aroused by Henry Cooke, won the day, we saw that many moderates remained within the mainline Presbyterian Church. It is such people who vote liberals into the professorships at the theological college and vote for continued membership of the World Council of Churches.

Over the Home Rule issues we see this moderation and liberalism coming to the surface again in the Ulster Liberal Association, which invited John Redmond, Joseph Devlin and Winston Churchill to a meeting in Belfast to speak about Home Rule. This was a courageous act in a city seething with defiance against the proposed Bill. In 1912, Churchill came and spoke in favour of the Bill at the Celtic Park football ground, which was in the Catholic area of the city. He was received with great cheers in that quarter, but had to run the gauntlet of Unionist and Orange opposition before he got there: unfortunately the weather was bad in addition to the place for the meeting having been badly chosen, and Churchill made a hurried and somewhat undignified exit from the province to escape their violence.[43] But the invitation showed that Unionists and Orangemen were not entitled to claim that they spoke for all Ulster people.

It is a truism that religion can be both a divisive and a cohesive force. Both aspects are apparent in Ulster. Thus the Catholics are bound together by their religion but by the same token divided from the Protestants. We have also seen the religious divide between Anglicanism and Presbyterianism, and it would appear that only Evangelical Protestantism or politics can bring them together. Hence denominations within a religion are divided by differences of doctrine and in the attitude to Church government. (This, needless to say, does not occur only in Christianity.) Arising from the religious differences in Ulster is the argument that Protestantism gives rise to capitalism. We have seen how industrial prosperity came to the North and not to the South: can it be maintained that this is somehow linked to the Protestant religion? Max Weber in his *The Protestant Ethic and the Spirit of Capitalism* maintained that the popular interpretation of Calvinism had been a major factor in the development of capitalism in the West; its adherents had sought economic success in a systematic way, believing it to be their vocation and offering a sign of elect status. Weber went too far in seeing religion producing economic factors, but the Calvinist and the Puritan did indeed stress individualism and an attitude to commerce that encouraged thrift and hard work, and frowned on pleasure.[44] This outlook is clearly present in the Ulster Protestants. Emphasis was placed on the massing of capital, and this was not difficult to do since their profits, according to their ethic, were not to be squandered on 'wine, women and song'. They were opposed to any lavishness of display either in their homes, in dress or in entertainment. What then could they do with their money but plough it back into their businesses and thus increase their capital? Certainly there was extraordinary industrial growth in Belfast after 1800, but it repelled visitors, from England especially, because of its stress on Calvinistic theology and its dedication to the Puritan ethic.

The economic prosperity of the North made its own contribution to religious strife. It encouraged Catholics not only from rural areas in the North but also from the South to come to work and settle. By 1850 the proportion of Catholics had reached 35 per cent, and the Protestants were alarmed. They lived apart from the Protestants, probably for reasons of both safety and convenience of worship, around the Falls Road in the west of the city. The Protestant area ran parallel to it; this was named the Shankill Road, hence, in the words of A.T.Q. Stewart, 'the proximity of these two communities divided by religion was the chief cause of the sporadic rioting, which was the worst blot on the city's good name.'[45]

We have seen some of the differences that arose between the Anglicans and Presbyterians concerning Church government and how these led at times to persecution, with the rejection of Presbyterian orders and the validity of its sacraments. There was basic agreement between the Anglicans and Presbyterians on doctrine, with theological splits, as we have seen, among the Presbyterians. But both were Reformed Churches, which meant that the theological differences dividing them from the Roman Catholics were much greater. Where do these disagreements lie and to what extent do they help us in trying to understand the outlook of the Ulster Protestant? We should note first of all that the three groups — Anglicans, Presbyterians and Catholics — were agreed on the doctrines of the Trinity and the Person of Christ. It was on the matter of salvation that they differed at the Reformation. The question then was: How can one be right with God? The Catholic answer was that the Church is central: 'No one can have God as father who does not have the Church as mother.' Without the Church, the priesthood and the seven sacraments, a person could not be saved, and only if one co-operated with the grace that flowed from these means was it possible to be delivered from one's sins. Luther denied such instrumental means, and his attack struck at the very heart of the system. Instead of seeing the Church as an extension of the Incarnation, as the Catholics did, he said that it was simply the bearer of the good tidings of the Gospel. He contended for the individual in relation to God without any priestly intermediary, and declared that all believers were priests. Such a doctrine was devastating in that it sought to overthrow the priestly and sacerdotal conception of the Church and abolish the medieval division between the sacred and the secular.

Luther retained the sacraments (to be precise, two of them — the communion and baptism) as signs, but other reformers went further and saw them only in terms of their psychological effects. Again, Luther thought of the grace of God in salvation as the promise and declaration of divine favour, without the co-operation of man, whereas the Catholic saw grace as a kind of spiritual infusion into the soul. Luther stressed justification by faith alone, and therefore attacked all the 'good works' that the Catholic Church insisted upon as being necessary for salvation. All these points and more were systematised by the legalistic Calvin in his famous work, *The Institutes of the Christian Religion*. It is clear that if such theology had been generally acceptable, the Catholic Church might have disintegrated. That it did not was due to the work of the Counter-Reformation, in which the Church set its house in order and corrected abuses but nevertheless retained its belief in the centrality of its institution, priesthood and sacraments.

In England the Reformation did not at first have the same devastating effect as on the continent. This was because it began on a question of supremacy by Henry VIII and only reached its full theological flowering through the work of Archbishop Cranmer and the practical enforcement by Elizabeth. But the number of martyrs under Queen Mary (1553–8) shows that the English in those days took their religion seriously, and refutes the charge sometimes made by the people of Ulster that the Church of England was never properly reformed. How is it, then, that the English fail to recognise the continued dominance of Reformed theology in Northern Ireland today? This is a key question in any understanding or misunderstanding of the Ulster Protestant.

A number of reasons might be suggested. First, the Protestant faith in England has not been interwoven with political events to the same extent as it is with the battle of the Boyne and the siege of Derry in the minds of Ulster Protestants. Secondly, the sharp historical and religious differences of the two faiths — the Catholic and the Reformed — have not been so continuously accentuated over the years as in Ireland. Thirdly, disloyalty to the Crown on the part of the Catholics has not (since the Revolution that ended the reign of James II, at least) been assumed and constantly stressed in England as it has in Ireland. Fourthly, the historic events that emphasise sectarian divisions are not still celebrated at the present time as they are in the North of Ireland. Fifthly, the English are not so easily aroused by theological controversy as the Ulster people and are more interested in practice than in theory. Sixthly, the ecumenical movement has had much greater force in England than in the North of Ireland, where the General Assembly of the Presbyterian Church decided to leave the World Council of Churches. Further, Christianity has encountered a tide of secularism and humanism in England that has not been experienced in Ulster. With this secularist trend, theology has been relegated to a minor place, where it has retained any place at all, in establishments of higher learning, and is only publicised when prominent churchmen such as the late John Robinson and David Jenkins seem to be deviating from traditional doctrine. Because barely ten per cent of people on the mainland attend worship, few have any knowledge of the theological issues involved. For average English people, the controversies between the Churches have long ceased to be of any great interest, and they only begin to take notice when Churches become involved in politics, or as when certain divines supported the coal miners in their 1984–5 strike, or appeared half-hearted over the British victory in the South Atlantic war of 1982. There is still an interest in religion on a global scale as reflected in the number of people enrolling for courses in general religious studies (as distinct from theology) and viewing programmes relating to it on television, but lack of knowledge of the Bible and of the finer points of theology go hand in hand.

In Ulster the religious atmosphere is markedly different. Churches are usually crowded, church advertising occupies several pages in every newspaper, theological sermons are preached, and the differences between the Reformed and the Catholic faiths are constantly underlined. Whereas England during the twentieth century has become an increasingly pluralist and secular society, Ulster still adheres strongly to a Christianity divided into Catholic and Protestant forms. Hence partition in 1921 was much more than the drawing of a geographical and physical boundary. It marked the difference in outlook of two faiths and two cultures, and this is further accentuated by the existence of these divisions within Ulster itself. J.C. Beckett admirably summed it up: 'The real partition of Ireland is not on the map but in the minds of men.'[46] How that partition has fared we consider in the next chapter.

REFERENCES

1. T.W. Moody and F.X. Martin (eds), *The Course of Irish History*, Cork: Mercier Press, 1976, p. 61.
2. J.C. Beckett, *A Short History of Ireland*, op. cit., p. 13.
3. E. Curtis, *A History of Ireland*, op. cit., p. 10. But Patrick introduced monasticism into Ireland, which meant that many important churches were ruled by monks rather than bishops (see Moody and Martin, op. cit., p. 65). Further there is evidence that the Irish Church developed its own ritual and traditions, independent of Rome; and there was no written correspondence between the Papacy and Irish Church leaders for over four centuries (640–1080). See Kenneth Neill, *An Illustrated History of the Irish People*, Dublin: Gill and Macmillan, 1979, p. 46.
4. Ibid., p. 18.
5. Ibid., p. 7.
6. Beckett, op. cit., p. 17.
7. Ibid., p. 47.
8. Ibid., p. 50.
9. Curtis, op. cit., p. 183.
10. Ibid., p. 229.
11. J.C. Beckett, *The Anglo-Irish Tradition*, London: Faber, 1976, p. 143.
12. F.S.L. Lyons, *Ulster: The Roots of Difference*, Oxford: Clarendon Press, 1979, p. 128.
13. Ibid.
14. Curtis, op. cit., p. 250.
15. Ibid., p. 275.
16. Ibid., p. 293.
17. Ibid., p. 306.
18. Beckett, op. cit., p. 99.
19. Ibid., p. 124.
20. Quoted by P. Berresford Ellis, *History of the Irish Working Class*, London: Gollancz, 1972, p. 77.

21. Curtis, op. cit., p. 332.
22. Robert Kee, *Ireland: A History*, op. cit., p. 61.
23. Beckett, op. cit., p. 127.
24. Ibid., p. 142.
25. Curtis, op. cit., p. 397.
26. Lyons, op. cit., p. 125.
27. J.M. Barkley, *A Short History of the Presbyterian Church in Ireland*, Belfast, 1959, p. 46.
28. R.G. Crawford, *Challenge and Conflicts*, Belfast: W. & G. Baird, 1981, p. 99.
29. *The Non-Subscribing Presbyterian*, Belfast, Sept. 1923, p. 5.
30. Barkley, op. cit., p. 46 Belfast.
31. R.F.G. Holmes, *Challenge and Conflict*, p. 125.
32. For complete analysis, ibid., p. 116ff.
33. E. Orr, *The Second Evangelical Awakening*, London: Marshall, Morgan & Scott, 1949, p. 176; See also Lyons, op. cit., p. 126.
34. Ibid., p. 205.
35. Lyons, op. cit., p. 141.
36. Ibid., p. 142.
37. Curtis, op. cit., p. 398.
38. Ibid., p. 399.
39. Ibid., pp. 380ff.
40. Beckett, op. cit., p. 154.
41. Stewart, op. cit., p. 61.
42. Ibid., p. 64.
43. Ibid., p. 54.
44. See R.H. Tawney's criticism of Weber in *Religion and the Rise of Capitalism*, London: John Murray, 1922, pp. 312–3.
45. Stewart, op. cit., p. 46.
46. Beckett, op. cit., p. 176.

4

THE RISE AND FALL OF STORMONT

Stormont, the Ulster government, began and ended in violence. In the fifty years of its existence it did not convert the Ulster Catholic to the British way of life — which, ironically, can be compared with the South's inability to attract the Ulster Protestant to the idea of a Republic. In fact, the full irony of Stormont is best appreciated by visiting the place: photographs do not adequately convey the impressiveness of its architecture and setting — clearly it was intended to last a thousand years, not just a few decades. It is our intention in this chapter not to retell the story of events of the period but to try and understand the attitudes and traits in the Ulster character which led to the present impasse. These attitudes, developed and hardened by past experience, were to lead to a political, religious and social apartheid, and eventually to the downfall of the state.

Stormont got off to a bad start, because from the beginning nobody really wanted it. The Catholics longed to be united with the Republic, and the Protestants had never demanded a parliament of their own. Indeed the Protestants reminded the British government of the sacrifices they had made in agreeing to self-government, and mourned the fact that Ireland as a whole had been allowed to relinquish its ties with the mainland. Only with the passing of time did the Unionists realise the advantages of having a parliament of their own.[1]

There was something very artificial about the Border itself in such a small country. No line drawn across a map can solve political problems, and in 1921 it was accepted that the Border constituted a temporary measure and a compromise in difficult negotiations. It set the precedent for the partition agreed for Palestine in 1936 and that of India in 1947. In none of the three cases has partition brought peace and social harmony.[2] Irish villages and farms had to be divided as the Border cut through them. The same farmer could be working in one field in the morning which was inside the 'Six Counties', and in the afternoon in another which was in the Free State; he could be having his breakfast in the North and sleeping the following night in the South.

That politics and religion were firmly joined together in Ulster was expressed with complete clarity in 1934 by the first Prime Minister, Sir James Craig (Lord Craigavon): 'I am an Orangeman first and a member of this particular parliament afterwards. . . . We are a Protestant parliament and a Protestant state.' With regard to the Catholics, Lord Brookeborough was blunt: 'Catholics are out to destroy Ulster with all their might and power. They want to nullify the Protestant vote to take all they can out of Ulster and then see it go to hell.'³ How could a member of a government speak of one-third of the people in his country as traitors? He could point to the Catholics' refusal to take their seats in the Ulster parliament in 1921. Indeed it was not till 1925, with the collapse of the Boundary Commission, that they participated — and their general attitude during those early years was one of non-cooperation and disobedience. Some Catholic teachers refused salaries, and their schools would not accept grants. Areas with a Catholic majority declared allegiance to the South, and local authorities pledged support to the Dáil in Dublin.⁴

It was not long before violence broke out, with the I.R.A. stirring up communal strife and engaging in murder. This brought into the field against them the 'B Specials', who became a force feared and hated by the Catholics. In 1922, as a result, the Special Powers Act was introduced, authorising the Minister of Home Affairs to take steps and issue orders necessary to maintain the peace. This virtually removed the individual's right of civil, political and personal liberty. The Minister could declare organisations illegal, detain people without charge or trial, impose curfews and restrict movement, prohibit inquests, and order searches and arrests without warrants. The Act, which was intended to be temporary, lasted till 1972!

The Catholics were discriminated against in the right to vote. The House of Commons of the Ulster parliament, according to the 1920 Act, was to be elected by a system of proportional representation, which was designed to safeguard the Catholic minority. This system of voting was opposed by the Ulster Unionists, and in 1929 Lord Craigavon abolished it in favour of the British system of single-member constituencies. Thus he had no problem in keeping the Unionist Party in power from 1921 till 1972.⁵ As John Magee says, 'There was one striking and fundamental difference between the Northern Ireland parliamentary system and that of the United Kingdom: one party was continually in office during the whole of its life, and the state's survival was thought to depend upon a continuance of that situation indefinitely. There was no possibility of the opposition coming into power or of the government going out; this encouraged irresponsibility on one side and arrogance on the other. Unionist politicians saw no need to obtain Catholic consent for the new institutions, and over a period of fifty years they were gradually alienated.'⁶

But this sense of superiority on the part of the Ulster Protestants hid their fears. They knew that the Government of Ireland Act of 1920 looked forward to the eventual unification of Ireland, and that it was intended to set up a Council of Ireland. Thus they feared not only the Catholics of the North, but also the South on the one hand and the British government on the other. This mentality continued with the insecure feeling that somebody, somewhere, was going to 'do a Lundy' on them (see above, p. 23). Even in one of the most heroic deeds of the Ulster Volunteer Force at the battle of the Somme in 1916, they had the feeling of being let down. Of this action Sir Wilfred Spencer said: 'I am not an Ulsterman, but yesterday as I followed their amazing attack on the Somme I felt that I would rather be an Ulsterman than anything else in the world.' Yet the Ulster people knew that if adequate support had been given by the British, they would not have suffered such extremely heavy casualties.⁷ They knew too how in 1689 the English ships had delayed before entering the port of Derry to relieve the siege; and they recalled the experience of the Penal Laws and how they had had to fight to preserve their position during the Home Rule issue. All of this contributed to make them mistrustful of the Anglo-Irish agreement signed at Hillsborough in 1985.

The Ulster Protestants fear the South and the Catholic Church there. Till recently the Dublin government did not accord even a partial recognition to the state of Northern Ireland, and has repeatedly claimed that it is part of the Irish state. The Republican areas of South Armagh ('bandit country'), Tyrone and South Derry have always believed this and actively campaigned for the end of partition. In 1937 Eamon De Valera inserted a clause in the Constitution of the Irish state that recognised the special position of the Catholic Church, and the influence was soon to be seen in every aspect of social life. Attitudes on both sides of the divide hardened with Sir James Craig's declaration in 1934 that there was a Protestant parliament and a Protestant state in Ulster, and De Valera countered in the Republic with the statement that Ireland was a Catholic nation.⁸ Indeed the insecurity felt by Ulster Protestants is better understood when it is realised that not till 1949 were they given a positive guarantee of the permanence of their state: 'It is hereby declared that Northern Ireland remains part of His Majesty's dominions and of the United Kingdom, and it is hereby affirmed that in no event will Northern Ireland or any part thereof cease to be part of His Majesty's dominions and of the United Kingdom without the consent of the Parliament of Northern Ireland.'⁹ Ever since, this guarantee has been an anchor to which the Ulster Protestant people have clung in a perilous sea of troubles.

We shall review the attitude of the Protestants in more detail later, but it is ironic in the light of the theological difference between the two communities that we noted in the last chapter to see at this point that a Catholic ethic was developing in Ireland during the 1920s and 1930s which closely resembled the Evangelical and Puritan ethic of the Ulster Protestant. It seemed that the celibate priest in the South was determined to impose upon his parishioners certain rules which would encourage if not compel celibacy. Films and literature were censored, drinking was frowned upon, dancing was regarded as liable to lead to illicit sex, and neither divorce nor birth control was permissible. Since many young men had to wait until their parents died before they could take possession of the family farm, they often either never married at all or did so only at a relatively late age. Pre-marital sexual intercourse was effectively prevented by the Church. These same things were all likewise discouraged and frowned upon by the Evangelical Protestant in the North and, apart from a more joyous celebration of Sunday in the Republic, the general ethical values began to look very similar.[10] But in theology and conduct of worship, and in culture, the gap was as wide as ever, for it was the intention of the new Republic to react against anything regarded as British.

Thus it initiated a revival of the Gaelic language and literature and laid emphasis on the teaching of the Catholic Church. The Ulster Protestant watched suspiciously as these ideas gained momentum among the Catholics of the North, and was further irritated by the law of the Catholic Church whereby all the children of a mixed marriage were to be brought up as Catholics. This regulation, made in Rome in 1908, has remained in force up to the present. We shall refer to it in more detail later.

Further, the Catholic Church had shown a tendency to discourage Southerners from fighting for the British in the World Wars. In 1915, Bishop Edward O'Dwyer of Limerick made this clear to John Redmond, head of the Irish Parliamentary Party, and in 1916 he defended the Easter rising. Other prominent churchmen followed his lead in encouraging the Irish Republic Brotherhood, later to be called the Irish Republican Army.[11] But it must be said that the Church moved to condemn the I.R.A. when the civil war broke out in the South, and ranged itself on the side of the Free State government. In particular, it 'denied the sacraments to active opponents of the government, which for the average Irish Catholic was the ultimate punishment since it placed his soul in everlasting jeopardy.'[12]

In 1972, the Republic took a step to try and allay the fear of the Ulster Protestants that Home Rule was Rome Rule by removing the 'special position' of the Catholic Church from its Constitution.[13] But in the same year Cardinal William Conway, Archbishop of Armagh, asserted that the majority was entitled to prevent the minority from doing things which might be permissible according to the latter's conscience if this should be necessary to prevent change or damage to the 'kind of society we have'. As for divorce, he said he was sure that the majority would reject a change in the existing prohibition if the issue went to a referendum. In this he was proved right in 1986. The Ulster Protestants, who have always argued for liberty of conscience, see this as a denial of their rights, and recognise that in a united Ireland they would be forced to do what the majority, relying on the authority of their Church, would insist upon.[14] This is a reasonable argument, yet the Ulster Protestants did not consider it contrary to their conscience, being in the majority in their own state, to engage in a process of discrimination which opposed the principles of democracy and equality. Such is the temptation of power to which a majority can succumb.

To revert to Catholicism, one of the greatest sources of division in the province was a decision taken by the Catholic Church, when the Education Act of 1923 was introduced in Northern Ireland, to maintain control of its schools. At a time when the Protestants were handing over their schools under certain conditions to the state, the Catholics successfully resisted such pressure, accepting in 1930 a 50 per cent grant from the state to continue as they were. This was later increased to 65 per cent under the 1944 Education Act (1947 in Northern Ireland), although the Catholics wanted parity with England — i.e. an 80 per cent grant.

Why did the Catholics refuse? They feared that their children might be given religious instruction by Protestant teachers; this would have been in opposition to their canon law, which states that 'nothing contrary to the Catholic religion be taught' to the children. Again, 'Catholic pupils are not to frequent non-Catholic schools. . . .' Only in rare cases would permission be granted for mixed schooling.[15] Whatever the rights or wrongs of the Catholic case, it perpetuated the social and sectarian division of the polity of Ulster. Only in technical schools and at Queen's University in Belfast could Protestants and Catholics meet, and it is significant that the Civil Rights Movement (C.R.M.) obtained some of its prominent leaders from that University. Although generalisations are dangerous, it is usually accepted that the Catholic schools stressed Irish history and the Irish language, whereas the state schools put the emphasis on British history. Hence my own ignorance of what happened in the South. Bernadette Devlin,* one of the leaders of the C.R.M., said that her high school was 'militantly Republican', with everything 'Irish-oriented', but she states that not all Catholic schools were as extreme as hers. However, Gary MacEoin notes that many were and continue to be so.¹⁶

The Protestants, for their part, while they conceded their schools to the state and endorsed mixed higher education at Queen's, discriminated over the siting of the New University of Ulster at Coleraine in 1968. The Catholics and Protestants of Derry both wanted the University to be established in their city, where Magee College already had buildings and students, but because the Catholics wanted it, the government would not even yield to Protestant demands from Derry for fear that the University would become a Catholic stronghold. As the Cameron Commission pointed out, 'this caused a degree of unity in resentment and protest which was probably unique, at least in the recent history of the city, and united local opinion in a suspicion that the central government was deliberately discriminating against the city and its interests for political reasons.' Magee, it should be noted, was originally a Presbyterian institution. As it turned out, the New University of Ulster did not succeed on its site at Coleraine, and was eventually amalgamated with the Polytechnic at Jordanstown, on the outskirts of Belfast. The Protestants failed to heal divisions in higher education, but the Catholics in turn had not adopted the positive attitude of one of their Bishops, James Doyle, Bishop of Kildare, with regard to their schools:

'I do not see how any man wishing well to the public peace, and who looks to Ireland as his country, can think that peace can be permanently established, or the prosperity of the country ever well secured, if children are separated at the commencement of life on account of their religious opinions. I do not know any measures which would prepare the way for a better feeling in Ireland than uniting children at an early age, and bringing them up in the same school, leading them to commune with one another and to form those little intimacies and friendships which subsist through life.'¹⁷

* Now Bernadette McAliskey, M.P. (Independent Unity) for Mid-Ulster, 1969–74, entering the House of Commons at the age of twenty-one.

Instead, the Catholics made sure that their hold on the children was strengthened by withdrawing a concession concerning the *Ne Temere* decree (see above, p. 54), which stated that the presence of a parish priest was necessary to make a marriage valid. But in the Netherlands in 1741 and Ireland in 1785, concessions had been made whereby marriages outside the Church of Rome, though considered sinful, were recognised. This concession was withdrawn in 1908 in Ireland. Thus, in a mixed marriage, both parties are required to sign a declaration with the following four points: (1) there shall be no interference with the religion of the Catholic party or his (or her) practice of it; (2) the Catholic party shall endeavour in every reasonable way to bring the non-Catholic party to the faith; (3) all the children of the marriage shall be baptised and brought up in the Catholic faith; and (4) the parties shall not present themselves either before or after the Catholic marriage before a non-Catholic minister of religion for any religious ceremony. The third of these stipulations, as Barritt and Carter point out, implies that the children must go to Catholic schools.[18]

If the Catholic Church was hardening attitudes by its policies, the same thing was happening on the Protestant side. Sir Basil Brooke (later Lord Brookeborough) openly admitted in 1933 that he would not employ Catholics in his business; and the Unionist party has always displayed utter determination not to be out-voted by Catholics. 'In practice', says the Ulster journalist Martin Wallace, 'this has meant at different levels a policy of restricting Catholics' opportunities — notably in employment and housing — so that population ratios and consequently political power remain fairly constant.'[19]

But nowhere is the Unionist inflexibility seen more clearly than on the Border question. In a pamphlet issued in 1956, leading members of the Unionist Party — Brookeborough, Brian Maginess, Robert Hanna — put forward the reasons why partition must always remain. Having stressed the slogans 'Not an inch' and 'No surrender', Brookeborough said that the Ulster state was preserved not by the British garrison but by the will of the people. This needed to be stated, since wild rumours were current in the United States that the British were in occupation of the North of Ireland. Maginess posed the question: Is it necessary to be anti-British in order to be Irish? Britain wronged America, but was now America's chief ally. Ulstermen fought for the independence of America, and in the rebellion of 1798 in Ulster, yet now they were united with Britain. It was the present, not the past, that was important for Ulster and America, but for the Republic the past was what mattered. Ideas made the difference between the North and the South. In the North there was freedom of thought and expression, but in the South there was censorship in various forms. Maginess, in these statements, could hardly have anticipated that freedom of speech and movement would be greatly curtailed as the Civil Rights movement developed in the 1960s, and that such legal enactments as the Special Powers Act would be enforced. Hanna stressed the economic links and deplored the tariffs imposed by the South on cross-channel trade; he also spoke of the identity of purpose which united Ulster with the United Kingdom and the United States in Western defence. And of course there was the royal allegiance of the province.[20]

Since it has so often been said that Northern Ireland is a captive of the past, it is interesting that this piece of Unionist propaganda argues that it is the South and not the North which is captive. Basically both are, for the Easter rising of 1916 is celebrated in the South just as the battle of the Boyne is in the North. Such celebrations not only inspire both sides to keep the past alive but inflame passions and renew hatreds.

Still, not all Unionists have sought to maintain the divide, and in December 1950, at the Young Unionist political school in Portstewart, County Londonderry, Sir Clarence Graham, chairman of the standing committee of the Ulster Unionist Council, said that he did not rule out the possibility that the day might come when many members of the Nationalist Party would wish to join the Unionist Party. Further, he thought that there was no reason why a Catholic should not be selected as a Unionist parliamentary candidate. Brian Maginess, whom we mentioned above, called for greater toleration and co-operation between all sections of the community. Since for Unionists 'Roman Catholic' meant 'Nationalist', this school at Portstewart with its liberal opinions was heavily criticised, and within a few days Sir George Clark, the Grand Master of the Orange Lodge of Ireland, made a speech asserting that under no circumstances would Catholics be admitted to membership of the Unionist party with the approval of the Orange Order; the liberty of the Unionist party, which was laid down in its constitution, was the liberty of the Protestant religion and excluded Catholics with their vastly different religious outlook. Lord Brookeborough bowed to these opinions and stated that the Portstewart speeches had been quite unnecessary.[21]

It was in this intolerant atmosphere that Terence O'Neill emerged as Prime Minister in 1963 and brought with him a refreshing wind of change. He described Lord Brookeborough as 'a man of limited intelligence ... in the hands of his dominating wife ... difficult to shake from some of his more idiotic ideas. The tragedy of his premiership was that he did not use his tremendous charm and his deep Orange roots to try and persuade his devoted followers to accept some reforms. In twenty years he never crossed the Border, never visited a Catholic school and never received or sought a civic reception from a Catholic town.'[22] O'Neill did all these things, and how he did them and how they were reported is significant. The press, anxious to make something sensational out of his visit to the Catholic school, photographed him from an angle that made the crucifix (the only thing which distinguished the school from a state school) appear directly above his head! This would scarcely have been noticed, let alone caused excitement, in England but to the Ulster Protestant the crucifix is seen purely as an emblem of Catholicism and, as such, anathema. On the death of Pope John XXIII, O'Neill sent a message of condolence to Cardinal Conway at Armagh, and the next day the headline in the newspaper was 'The Pope: Ulster Premier's message'. Since this acknowledgement of the Pope, who was regarded as the 'anti-Christ', was accompanied by the flying of the flag over the City Hall at half-mast (it was only a month before the celebration of the glorious victory over Catholicism at the battle of the Boyne), the extremists were further incensed.[23]

O'Neill, a moderate, was treading the way of reasonable compromise, but he was doing so in the context of Protestant bigotry and personal ambition among his ministerial colleagues in the Ulster parliament. His determination to reform abuses came up against parochial and unchangeable minds. Yet it needs to be said, especially in the light of the later worsening of the crisis, that general opinion was with him, even after the visit of the Prime Minister of the Republic, Sean Lemass, to Belfast. This was shown by the election of 1965, which he won. Moderates were then in the majority, and wished the good relations and community feeling which O'Neill was fostering to be continued. He was criticised for the unheralded nature of Lemass's visit but, as he explains, it was necessary to keep much of the details secret to ensure the Taoiseach's safety. Further, he says that he had consulted his most senior ministers and the Governor of Northern Ireland, Lord Erskine, who had approved.[24]

That O'Neill's work was appreciated by the Catholics was shown when he visited Catholic areas, both in Belfast and in the country (later scenes of the worst rioting), during election campaigns and was well received and applauded for his reforms. Apart from his activity at home, which was a trail-blazing effort, he was an excellent ambassador: he organised 'Ulster Weeks' throughout England, advertising the province, and he scored a number of firsts: the first meeting between a Northern Ireland Prime Minister and the President of United States, the first visit to Northern Ireland of the Prime Minister of the Republic, and the first official visit to West Germany.

O'Neill's reforms and suggestions bemused Westminster. Harold Macmillan reacted to his suggestion that President Kennedy should visit Ulster by asking him why he wanted to make himself unpopular with Ulster Protestants. And Harold Wilson said: 'Why are you pursuing a policy which is so unpopular with the Protestants when you could for instance have decided not to meet Mr Lemass?' Economic co-operation was the reason for the latter, and a visit by Kennedy would have delighted the Catholics and would not have been opposed by the moderate Protestants. Not surprisingly, O'Neill also received little support from the Protestant clergy, and at times was condemned too by the Catholic Church, when he mentioned the divisiveness of separate education. Still, on the matter of education he was supported by certain Nationalist M.P.s, in opposition to the Catholic Church.[25]

Time and again O'Neill tried to arouse moderate opinion. He argued that to be British was to have an innate sense of justice and fair play, and he called for wisdom, fairness and patriotism in the province. It was necessary to seek the 'middle ground', which could be occupied by all reasonable people.[26] But eventually, either through intimidation or apathy, the moderates let him down. He responded to the Civil Rights Movement and agreed to its demands by establishing a commission for Londonderry which would have ensured fair house allocation, the appointment of an ombudsman, and other measures. Indeed one of his last acts in office was to force through its basic demand for 'one man, one vote' in local elections. For the extremists moderation was treason, and yet he even addressed his appeals to them: 'The bully-boy tactics we saw in Armagh are no answer to these grave problems; but they incur for us the contempt of Britain and the world, and such contempt is the greatest threat to Ulster. Let the government govern and the police take care of law and order.'[27]

Criticised for not establishing Ulster's New University at Derry, O'Neill pointed out that both the University and Ulster's projected 'new city' of Craigavon had been sited on the objective advice of recognised experts, Dr Robert Matthew and Sir John Lockwood, neither of whom had any connection with Northern Ireland or had been influenced by his government. His attitude to religion reflected this moderation too. Religion was for him a private affair, not to be mixed with politics; at the most, it should enrich politics. Ulster, instead, was debasing Christianity with its brand of politics. 'We seem to have forgotten that love of neighbour stands beside love of God as a fundamental principle of our religion. I was moved, as many of you must have been, to see the leading clergy of Derry, Protestant and Roman Catholic, side by side in the streets of that troubled city. This simple act of Christian friendship was a shining example of what would have been possible, but for the machinations of wicked men who have preached and practised hatred in the name of God.'[28] He commended clergy who quietly inculcated such virtues in their flock and did not engage in publicity-seeking marches and countermarches. Such sentiments, expressed in various speeches, evoked a flood of support for his changes, and the Civil Rights leaders declared a period of truce at the end of 1968. Then extremists like the People's Democracy, a left-wing organisation, broke the truce with marches in January 1969 to such sensitive places as Derry and Newry. Rioting and violence followed.

Extremists on the Protestant side argued that O'Neill's reforms and friendship with the South were the 'thin edge of the wedge' on the road to a united Ireland. But although O'Neill had been friendly and wanted to co-operate with the South, he was ready to criticise any efforts by the Republic to undermine Ulster's position within the United Kingdom. At a meeting of the Commonwealth Parliamentary Association at Westminster on 4 November 1968, he pointed out that the Irish Free State in 1925 had accepted both the Border and the existence of a legitimate parliament and government in Northern Ireland. But Eamon De Valera had ignored this Agreement and promulgated in 1937 a new constitution which laid claim to the whole of Ireland. The Free State also defaulted on its treaty obligations with the British, and initiated a 'trade war' by erecting a high tariff barrier on the Border. Goods passing from the South to the North came in duty-free, but trade coming from the North to the South was subjected to a high tariff. Added to this, I.R.A. terrorism, based on the South, continued to destroy life and property in the North, and then the neutrality of the Free State during the Second World War and the declaration of an Irish Republic in 1948 brought about the final breach with Britain and the Commonwealth. These statements by O'Neill are important, for they reveal, better than the more impassioned statements of extremists, how the sense of grievance of the Ulster Protestants (which he shared) was maintained. If the English find it impossible to understand the Ulster Protestants and see them as stiff and forever on the defensive, it is because their own 'Britishness' has never been put under the same pressure as has been experienced by the North of Ireland.[29]

However, despite the clarity of O'Neill's speeches and the obvious sincerity of his approach, the extremists still professed to believe that he was intent on a 'sell-out' to the South. Ian Paisley in particular attacked both what he saw as the Romeward trend of the mainline Protestant Churches and O'Neill's planned reforms of Stormont. His slogan was 'O'Neill must go'. Paisley represented all those negative qualities which we have seen emerging in the development of the Ulster character: siege mentality, fear and insecurity, refusal of all compromise, prejudice, a parochial outlook. . . . Ready to pounce on the least hint of liberalism, he was able to rally those Protestants whose outlook was narrow and education limited. In the early 1960s he fished energetically in Ulster's increasingly troubled waters. In 1964 he demanded the removal of the Irish tricolour flag from the window of the offices of the Republican Party, Sinn Fein, in Belfast; the Royal Ulster Constabulary (R.U.C.) obeyed him and twice broke in to remove the flag. This ignited the worst riots in the Falls Road since 1935. His protests against the ecumenical trend in the Presbyterian Church led to clashes with Catholics in the Cromac Square area, and provoked O'Neill's comment of 'Nazi gangsterism'. Paisley was arrested and sent to jail for three months.

Paisley is an orator with strong personality, commanding presence and unflinching dogmatism. His followers, who are mainly drawn from the 'grass-roots', have a narrow perspective and he is able to exploit this weakness to the full. But he is also an able organiser. Having founded his newspaper the *Protestant Telegraph* in 1966, he quickly proceeded to rally the Loyalists by forming the Ulster Constitution Defence Committee. He had little formal education apart from some theological instruction, and received no qualifications from recognised universities or training by any of the mainline Churches; thus he is virtually self-taught compared with the leaders of other denominations. The latter have taken great pains to avoid conflict with him: 'Without being a member of the Loyal Orange Institution, Paisley probably has more influence on much of its membership than is exercised by the hierarchy of the order; not an Official Unionist, he has upstaged that Party and broken its half-century of political monopoly; he has built up the Free Presbyterian Church of Ulster largely from membership of the Presbyterian Church in Ireland. As a M.P. he works impartially (not including the 'disloyal' Catholics!) and effectively for his constituents, and has consolidated a broad base of political power. In the Presbyterian General Assembly those who oppose the ecumenical movement deny that they are influenced by Paisley, and this may be accepted; but many of those they count as their followers are really following the Paisley line.'[30] If a former Moderator of the General Assembly of the Presbyterian Church of Ireland (the Rt Revd Austin Fulton) can pay such a compliment to Paisley, a Catholic bishop sees him as the force which prevents dialogue with his Church: 'Any Protestant churchman or politician who shows any sense of rapprochement or willingness to come closer with members of the Catholic Church will usually find that it is the prelude to the end of his career.'[31]

When the record of the Churches during the O'Neill period is considered, it is apparent that Paisley had a growing influence. They tried hard to move towards dialogue, but the growing ecumenism was thwarted by the fears of Paisley and the conservative elements within the Churches. Dialogue between Catholic and Protestant Church people had begun as far back as 1964 and conferences were held annually, but it was noted that attendance among the laity was low.[32] Catholic power and the doctrine of the infallibility of the Pope remained stumbling-blocks, but in 1966 the (Anglican) Church of Ireland could speak of sectarianism being outmoded,[33] and at the start of the riots valiant efforts were made by all the Churches to maintain peace and promote reconciliation. Here was moderation in religion caught between the Paisleyite extremists and the Civil Rights marchers. The moderates on the Protestant side called for meetings with the Catholic hierarchy to restore community relations, stressed restraint, and requested the Prime Minister to set up a commission of inquiry (the Cameron Commission) into the grievances of the minority in the North. The head of the Roman Catholic Church in Ireland, Cardinal Conway, acknowledged their work for the cause of social justice, but he was criticised by the Moderator of the Presbyterian Church and other Church leaders for not acknowledging that his own Catholic people had also contributed to the 'malaise of Ulster'.[34]

Practical and humanitarian service was rendered by the Churches during these troubles, and they opened their halls to the homeless, established peace committees, patrolled the streets at night, calmed fears, and at times physically occupied ground between opposing mobs.[35] While Paisley responded on occasion to the pleas of the moderate clergy to call off demonstrations or to use his influence to persuade mobs to disperse, he generally continued his work of denouncing any contact between

Catholic and Protestant clergy or politicians. When the Presbyterian Assembly was held in Dublin in 1969, it was visited by President De Valera, and this gave Paisley the opportunity of attacking the Moderator of the Assembly (the Rt Revd Dr John T. Carson) for 'grasping the hand of a murderer'.[36]

From the 1960s up to the present time, Paisley has challenged the liberalism of Ulster politicians and questioned the theological orthodoxy of Anglicans, Presbyterians Methodists and Catholics. He was successful in enticing many mainline Presbyterians into his Free Presbyterian Church, and had new church buildings put up all over the province. A skilled rabble-rouser, he baited the Catholics, obstructed the marches of the Civil Rights Movement, and brought wrath down on the head of O'Neill by declaring that in entertaining Sean Lemass he had taken to his bosom a 'Fenian Papist murderer'. The reference was to Lemass's participation in the Anglo-Irish war from 1919 to 1921.

Paisley's utterances led others to violence: most notably the Ulster Volunteer Force (U.V.F.). This body took its name from Edward Carson's paramilitary force, and used methods similar to those of the I.R.A. This was the 'dark underbelly' of Ulster life, and in 1966 its members committed a number of sectarian murders on the eve of the visit by Queen Elizabeth II to commemorate the sacrifice of Ulster soldiers at the battle of the Somme exactly fifty years before.[37] The existence of the U.V.F. demonstrates that force and violence are not far beneath the surface of Ulster Protestantism, although it is argued that it was only in reaction to the murders by the I.R.A. that the U.V.F. began its activity. But innocent people were killed in its operations against the I.R.A., and it was declared illegal under the Special Powers Act. In the state of unrest that then existed in the province, one scarcely dares to think what kind of backlash might have come from the mainland if the concrete block thrown at the Queen's car had landed on and gone through the roof and not merely damaged the bonnet. A young Catholic worker was arrested for the crime.

Of course, one of the immediate reasons for the unrest in the 1960s was discrimination. The Catholics protested against gerrymandering in local elections; 'The technique of the gerrymander is to draw constituency or ward boundaries in such a way that you spread your own support as thin as you dare over as many seats as possible, while you crowd your opponents' support into as few seats as possible.'[38] Thus in Derry, 80 per cent of 14,325 Catholics (1966) were placed in one ward which returned eight seats, while 87 per cent of the much smaller

Protestant population (9,235) were put into two wards which returned twelve seats. Year after year, there was a Protestant and a Unionist majority of twelve to eight on the city Corporation. This technique was applied throughout Ulster, and given great force by the business vote which allowed limited companies to nominate up to six extra voters (usually Protestants). Further, only resident and general occupiers of houses could vote, which meant that sub-tenants, lodgers, servants and youths over twenty-one living at home (about 250,000) were disfranchised.[39] No wonder the world was startled by the Civil Rights slogan 'One man, one vote'. It seemed incredible that in any part of the United Kingdom in the second half of the twentieth century many people did not possess the vote for local government elections. Again, as was pointed out by the Cameron Commission on Disturbances in Northern Ireland in 1969, the possibility of Catholics getting jobs and housing with these Protestant local councils was minimal.

A survey published by the Campaign for Social Justice in 1969 showed that in public employment there was a predominance of Protestants in senior positions covering such fields as the health services, the police, the administration of justice, the schools inspectorate and the administrative, professional and technical grades of the civil service.[40] It was also notable that of the 10,000 workers in the Belfast shipyard, the biggest single employer in the city, just 400 were Catholics. The O'Neill administration held out the promise of gradual reform and better economic development through co-operation with the South, but the events of the Civil Rights movement precipitated a conflict between the more radical elements of society. Even if this had not occurred, his programme had split the Unionist party, whose majority were in favour of maintaining the *status quo*.

In the 1960s violent student protests were seen in many countries of the Western world, and it was in 1967, as we have seen, that the Civil Rights movement was founded in Ulster. The two happenings had in common that they were part of the spirit of the time. But, peaceful at first, the Civil Rights activists soon found themselves in conflict with the militant Protestants. Education had raised the young Catholics' hopes as more and more of them graduated from Queen's University in Belfast, but these hopes were dashed as they experienced discrimination in employment and housing. Even a few years earlier, in 1964, middle-class and professional Catholics had formed the Campaign for Social Justice, but the only result they had seen for their efforts was the agreement by the state to abolish the business vote for local elections. Now their demands escalated under the banner of the C.R.A., and became 'One man, one vote', the removal of gerrymandered boundaries, laws against discrimination by local government, the provision of machinery to deal with complaints, allocation of council housing on a points system, the repeal of the Special Powers Act, and the disbanding of the 'B Specials'.

As marches and counter-marches took place, violence erupted, and television, always interested in the sensational, alerted a worldwide audience to what was happening. And it was happening in a place which was so little known that many viewers did not know the names of the principal towns. We need not go into the details of what happened. Rather we should reflect on what Ian Paisley said when he met Bernadette Devlin in his home. He conceded that there might be injustices, but he remarked: 'I would rather be British than fair.' He appeared to be interpreting the concept of Britishness as maintaining the link with the Crown at all costs, whereas for many of less extreme opinion the term also has the implication of being just, impartial in judging right and wrong, and helping the underdog.

Neither Paisley nor the right wing of the Unionist Party could countenance the British way, which would have been to find a compromise between the demands of the Civil Rights movement and the *status quo*. Instead, they contended that the one-party state had to be preserved or, to put it in the terms of their slogans, 'Not an inch' and 'No surrender'. Attitudes polarised as the violence increased, and Civil Rights reform became changed into the demand for an all-Ireland socialist republic. The standard-bearer for this demand was People's Democracy, led by Bernadette Devlin, Michael Farrell and Eamon McCann. It had the support of the Labour Party in Britain, but Stormont saw the movement as a front for the I.R.A. A more objective view is that it had the support of the I.R.A., which nonetheless did not control it.[41]

O'Neill called for civil responsibility as well as civil rights, and the government prosecuted Paisley for illegal demonstrations and he was jailed; but Brian Faulkner, the Minister of Commerce, resigned in protest at the lack of strong government. Because he was a hardliner and soon to become Prime Minister of Northern Ireland, it is interesting to reflect on his defence of the Ulster state. The reason for Faulkner's resignation was the insistence by O'Neill on the appointment of the Cameron Commission to inquire into and report on the violence. This, Faulkner pointed out, would be interpreted as an abdication of government responsibility for the violence, and would place the state in the position of appearing to be forced to grant reforms against its will. He recorded his amazement at the bitterness of O'Neill's reply to his letter of resignation, a reply which suggested that he was playing a devious political game as part of a scheming, disloyal and ambitious strategy.[42]

The personal conflict between Faulkner and O'Neill highlighted the divisions that had grown up within the Unionist Party, which under Brookeborough had maintained a remarkable unity and stability. But the Catholics were now much more articulate, and their growing middle class of teachers, lecturers, accountants, solicitors and businessmen were no longer content with second-class citizenship. O'Neill, with his support dwindling, resigned, and Faulkner later recorded the following comment: 'Terence O'Neill was a hard-working Prime Minister who had much to contribute to Northern Ireland. He had a certain flair for publicity and for saying the right things. . . . but I do not think he ever felt at home in Ulster politics. His personal remoteness made it difficult for him to lead his party along new and difficult paths at a very critical period. . . .'[43] This certainly contains some truth. O'Neill admitted to the bad housing and unemployment but argued that much prosperity had been achieved, and that Protestant and Catholic were both much better off under the present dispensation in Ulster than if they had been in a united Ireland. Education, social services, housing and employment were expanding, and tourism was booming with a first-class network of roads throughout the province. A complete review of local government had been announced in 1966, which would have dealt with the grievances of the Civil Rights Association, but the movement was used by the I.R.A. to increase violence, and the extreme Protestant backlash came on to the streets as the result. The 'One man, one vote' slogan gave the impression that the state had made it illegal for Catholics to vote in elections to the Westminster and Stormont parliaments — which of course was not so; in actual fact, it only referred to the ratepayer's franchise in local elections.

O'Neill himself, in one of his most important statements, related his failure to the fears of the Ulster Protestant:

The basic fear of the Protestants in Northern Ireland is that they will be outbred by the Roman Catholics. It is frightfully hard to explain to a Protestant that if you give Roman Catholics a good job and a good house they will live like Protestants, because they will see neighbours with cars and television sets. They will refuse to have 10 children, but if the Roman Catholic is jobless and lives in a most ghastly hovel, he will rear 10 children on national assistance. It is impossible to explain this to the militant Protestant because he is so keen to deny civil rights to his Roman Catholic neighbours. He cannot understand, in fact, that if you treat Roman Catholics with due consideration and kindness they will live like Protestants in spite of the authoritative nature of their Church.[44]

Here O'Neill equates prosperity and better living conditions with what in fact amounts to a change in the religious attitude of the Catholics. In this he is too optimistic, if what we have said about the Catholic Church in this and other chapters is correct. The Catholics, prosperous or not, are extremely reluctant to oppose the teaching of their Church, which forbids them contraception and other 'unnatural' means of preventing the birth of children. They stand fast against both abortion and divorce, as the 1986 referendum on the divorce issue revealed to a somewhat astounded Dr Garret Fitzgerald, Prime Minister of the Republic. But O'Neill was right to point to the injustice of the Ulster Protestants in refusing civil rights to the Catholics; this was a betrayal not only of being British but of the Presbyterian forefathers who fought in the ranks of the United Irishmen for equality and justice for all the people of Ireland. What gave the men of violence on the Catholic side their tacit support was the unattractive image of Protestant Ulster which television carried into homes all over Britain. What was the British public to make of the antics of the obstructive Paisley, the obstinacy of the Minister of Home Affairs, William Craig (whom O'Neill had to dismiss), and the ambition of Faulkner? Extreme Protestant groups such as the U.V.F. and the U.P.A., stressing force on the one hand and the glorious Protestant heritage on the other, converted an already unattractive image into a very ugly one. In this situation even Harold Wilson (British Prime Minister, 1964–70 and 1974–7) admitted that the use of the Special Powers Act was necessary. 'No government in the world would have gone on with what was proposed [dispensing with these powers] until they were assured that there would be a period of law, order, peace and calm and quiet.'[45]

We have noted Faulkner's opinion of O'Neill, and this is confirmed by Lord Longford: 'The very fact that he felt apparently so much kinship with me made me realise how difficult it must be for him to feel at home as Prime Minister of Northern Ireland.' His aristocratic background, Eton education and service with the Brigade of Guards did not equip him for the Ulster political scene, but it seems unfair, in the light of the reforms he carried through, that the Civil Rights activists should have said that behind his facade of liberalism he was shoring up the sectarian *status quo*;[46] Indeed, as we have seen, he got into trouble because of his efforts to bridge the sectarian divide. James Callaghan's judgement is much more just than Faulkner's: 'O'Neill would have made an excellent prime minister in the conservative tradition in easier times. He had a genuine distaste for the narrow-minded sectarianism of Ulster politics and was the first Northern Ireland politician in the Ulster Unionist party to recognise that the province had to take into account the world that lay beyond its own borders.'[47]

There is, however, another point of view that has not been explored but could be put forward in the light of what we have said in previous chapters about the Protestant Anglican ascendancy. O'Neill projected the image and ethos of that ascendancy. His speeches were excellent, but his manner was condescending and at times autocratic. Despite what he has said about consulting certain people before the visit of Lemass, the fact remains that the majority of his cabinet only learned of the visit when Lemass was already on his way to Belfast. This offended the democratic Presbyterian outlook which is so strongly ingrained in Ulster Protestants: they demand to be consulted. There had been a time when what representatives of the ascendancy said would have been accepted without question, but in the 1960s such traditional authority was not only being questioned — it was being overthrown.

Still in defence of O'Neill, we know that when a 'man of the people' such as Brian Faulkner was given a chance, he fared still worse. Of course the situation he inherited was more critical. Faulkner was a hardliner, and showed this in 1967 when he criticised O'Neill for dismissing the Minister for Agriculture, Harry West, who had been opposed to O'Neill's policies of moderation, reconciliation and reform. Faulkner reinstated West when he became Prime Minister in 1971. O'Neill also dismissed William Craig, another extremist, who was to establish Vanguard, a paramilitary force. There is some evidence that Faulkner was opposed to the ecumenical movement in the Churches, and willing to work with Paisley;[48] and when internment was introduced under his rule, it proved to be a fatal mistake. But local security had suffered a severe blow under Major James Chichester-Clark, O'Neill successor, who had disarmed the Royal Ulster Constabulary (R.U.C.) and disbanded the 'B Specials'. In spite of their defects, these forces knew the local situation much better than the army, and in many ways could deal more effectively with the I.R.A. In their place the Ulster Defence Regiment was introduced. After internment this force had very few Catholics in it and indeed contained many former 'B specials'.

But Faulkner had the Orange Order and the majority of the Unionist Party behind him, and he went about his work in his accustomed businesslike way. If O'Neill had given the impression of being a dominator and Chichester-Clark at times of being a poor leader, Faulkner was accused of being a double-talker. Certainly he tried to please both sides. He satisfied the Protestant hardliners with internment and later the Catholics with power-sharing. Perhaps it would be kinder to him to argue that he possessed the political skill of flexibility, and changed to meet situations that arose. Thus it is on record that in 1969 it appeared to him inconceivable that Catholics should sit in the Stormont parliament, but in 1974 he was loud in his praise of the loyalty and co-operation of the Catholic Gerry Fitt of the Social Democratic and Labour Party (S.D.L.P.) and others.[49]

Faulkner did try to work with the Catholics, and in 1971 he appointed to his Cabinet the first Catholic ever to serve in that capacity in Northern Ireland, Dr Gerald Newe; he was made a Minister of State in Faulkner's own office without specific responsibility.[50] But trouble on the streets defeated Faulkner. The Social Democratic and Labour Party withdrew from Stormont as riots swept through Derry in 1971, and when thirteen demonstrators were shot dead there by the army on 30 January 1972 ('Bloody Sunday'), the death-knell sounded for Stormont.

Edward Heath, the British Prime Minister, informed Faulkner that his own government intended henceforward to control security in Northern Ireland, but Faulkner answered that he and his Cabinet could not accept this and would resign. Heath was quick to accept the offer of resignation, and thus committed the British government to finding a solution which would ensure for the minority as well the majority an active role in the life and affairs of the province. Thus, as we remarked at the start of this chapter, Stormont, born out of compromise in 1920, ended as it had begun — in violence.

Various reasons have been put forward for this, and some of them have emerged in our quest to understand the attitudes and motives inherent in the minds of Ulster Protestants. Most are opposed to any form of Republicanism, and deny the I.R.A claim that Ulster is held by the British army. Since they have freely chosen to remain with Britain, no terrorist organisation is going to make them relinquish this union. Thus they are to be admired for withstanding a breakdown of law and order such as would never have been tolerated in any other part of the United Kingdom. They also deny the Marxist analysis of the situation, namely that British capitalists (the bourgeoisie) have exploited both Protestant and Catholic workers and favoured the former to the detriment of the latter. Commitment to religious belief — instead of being manipulated, as the Marxist alleges, to keep the two communities divided — is a determining factor in the division. Ulster Protestants say that they are different from the Irish Catholic also because their respective cultures are different. We have looked at this in some detail, and merely note here that this 'Irish' culture, as distinct from the British, covers the broad spectrum of language, history, sport (apart from rugby and soccer), literature, music and religion.

The extreme Ulster Protestants are suspicious of Westminster, as they were of any politician at Stormont who, in the effort to create reconciliation between the two communities, tried to give the Catholics the rights and place which they regard as theirs. Such programmes, they think, are a front for the eventual unification of Ireland. Thus they saw the O'Neill reforms as giving the Catholics political and social equality, and this 'was tantamount to giving them the ascendancy. This Loyalist intransigence, rather than any uncontrollable bias to violence, pushed the Northern Ireland Civil Rights Association into the arms of the resurgent I.R.A.'[51] The same intransigence spoiled dialogue with the Catholic Church, and attacked any Protestant minister suspected of advocating membership of the World Council of Churches. 'The religious cause was "No Popery" and the political cause was "No surrender", the total effect was no change, no progress, no reconciliation, no hope.'[52] But the failure of the initiatives of Terence O'Neill can also be laid at the door of the moderate Ulster Protestants. At the beginning and for part of his administration, O'Neill's reforms were welcomed by the moderates but, whether through intimidation by the extremists or the apathy of hopelessness, the support faded. The lack of development of the Alliance Party, composed of Protestant and Catholic liberals, demonstrates this.

There were many causes for unrest during the period of Stormont government: the unemployment of the 1930s, the unfavourable treatment meted out to the Catholics, the social and educational divisions, the flag-waving and marches, the cultural gap — but the main causes, which remain to the present day, were politics and religion. The two combine together in the Orange Order. Since it was founded in 1795, the Order has been dedicated to ensuring Protestant domination and the union with Britain, which in effect has meant one-party rule. It transcended class, banding together small farmers and aristocratic landowners, factory workers and factory owners, shipyard craftsmen and their employers. At the beginning of the twentieth century it was estimated that some two-thirds of the male Protestant population were members of the Order. Each of its lodges has a chaplain, and the Grand

Master is a Presbyterian minister. In its essential make-up it is unique in the United Kingdom,[53] although it has a distinct if superficial resemblance to the Afrikaner Broederbond in South Africa (see below, Chapter 6). Its stance is defensive: to protect the Protestant homeland against the Catholic South and to resist those Catholics in the North who support the South's claims to the North. Religiously it is 'a bulwark against the imperialism of Rome on the one hand, and a defence of the purity of the Christian faith against the errors of Popery on the other'.[54]

Clergymen or politicians who appear to be straying from these objectives are in danger of losing their jobs. Changes in religion are very difficult in any society, but in Ulster, which is basically conservative, they can occasion splits and divisions in Churches. The area of politics is especially sensitive, since change can be construed as a threat to the link with Britain. From the beginning of the Northern Island state, Unionist politicians have been careful to keep their relations with the Orange Order in good repair. This was underlined when Brian Faulkner asserted that the Unionist Party relied upon the Orange Order and the Order trusted the Party; together they were an invincible combination.[55] In practice politicians often took the leaders of the Order into their confidence, and they used the Order, with its regular rallies and speeches, to support the state. Problems and questions of a critical nature were discussed in advance of the Twelfth of July parades and speeches, so that nothing critical of the government might be said in public.

With its politically divisive and sectarian character and its aggressive parades and demonstrations, the Orange Order stands in the way of any serious change in the North of Ireland. Its rallies are a spur for street riots, and its dogged belief that it should be allowed to march anywhere in the land — the sign of ownership — causes conflict with Catholics and, since the troubles began, with the British security forces. Captive to the past, its banners exult in the battle of the Boyne and the victory of the Protestants over the Catholics. Such tribal rites are intended to serve the parallel purposes of arousing passion for the Protestant supremacy and 'keeping the memory green'. As Macaulay wrote in the 1840s, 'Five generations have passed away and still the wall of Londonderry is to the Protestants of Ulster what the trophy of the Marathon was to the Athenians.'

It is clear that change and reform, even though seen to be very necessary by the 1960s, would be very unwelcome in the eyes of the Orange Order. Thus, in summary, reforms annoyed the Loyalists, aroused the expectations of the Catholics and spurred the Civil Rights Movement to demand a faster pace of change. The gunmen on both sides turned demonstrations which had at first been peaceful to their own advantage and, in the crisis of security that resulted, Westminster assumed direct control. Would William Whitelaw, Merlyn Rees and other peacemakers from the government in London be able to change what some were beginning to think was unchangeable: the mind of the Ulster Protestant?

REFERENCES

1. John Magee, *Northern Ireland: Crisis and Conflict*, London: Routledge & Kegan Paul, 1974, p. 11.
2. T. Downing (ed.), *The Troubles*, p. 98.
3. Magee, op. cit., p. 4.
4. Downing, op. cit., p. 97.
5. Magee, op. cit., p. 62.
6. Ibid., p. 63.
7. Gary MacEoin, *Northern Ireland: Captive of History*, New York: Holt, Rinehart and Winston, 1974, p. 291. Wilfred Spencer was a highly promising young officer in the British army, who harmed his prospects by signing the Covenant in 1912. He was later first secretary to the Stormont cabinet.
8. Lyons, op. cit., p. 152.
9. Martin Wallace, *Northern Ireland*, Newton Abbot, Devon: David and Charles, 1971, p. 26.
10. Lyons, op. cit., p. 152.
11. MacEoin, op. cit., pp. 165ff.
12. Ibid., p. 190.
13. Ibid., p. 291.
14. Ibid., p. 292.
15. Barritt and Carter, op. cit., p. 83.
16. MacEoin, op. cit., p. 46.
17. Barritt and Carter, op. cit., p. 79.
18. Ibid., p. 26.
19. Wallace, op. cit., p. 71.
20. *Why the Border Must Be*, issued by the Northern Ireland Government, 1956.
21. Wallace, op. cit., p. 72.
22. MacEoin, op. cit., p. 32.
23. Terence O'Neill, *Autobiography*, London: Rupert Hart-Davies, 1972, pp. 50, 59.
24. Ibid., p. 70.
25. Ibid., p. 79.
26. Ibid., p. 130.
27. Ibid., p. 145.
28. Ibid., p. 200.
29. Ibid., pp. 168ff.

30. A.A. Fulton, 'Church in Tension . . .', in *Challenge and Conflict*, Belfast: W. & G. Baird, 1981, p. 188.
31. Bishop of Derry, quoted in *Challenge and Conflict*, op. cit., p. 188.
32. Gallaher and Worrall, *Christians in Ulster, 1968–1980*, Oxford University Press, 1982, p. 30.
33. Ibid., p. 35.
34. Ibid., p. 48.
35. Ibid., p. 50.
36. Ibid., p. 48.
37. Downing, *The Troubles*, p. 134.
38. The *Sunday Times* 'Insight' Team, *Ulster*, Harmondsworth: Penguin Books, 1972, p. 34.
39. Ibid., p. 35.
40. Wallace, op. cit., p. 117.
41. MacEoin, op. cit., 225.
42. Brian Faulkner, *Memoirs of a Statesman*, London: Weidenfeld and Nicolson, p. 52.
43. Ibid., p. 53.
44. *Belfast Telegraph*, 5 May 1969.
45. Faulkner, op. cit., p. 112.
46. Lord Longford and Anne McHardy, *Ulster*, London: Weidenfeld and Nicolson, 1981, p. 104.
47. Ibid., p. 116.
48. A. Boyd, *Brian Faulkner*, Tralee, Co. Kerry: Anvil Books, 1972, pp. 28, 57.
49. Longford and McHardy, op. cit., p. 137.
50. Ibid., p. 149.
51. Ibid., p. 129.
52. Ibid., p. 20.
53. J. Hickey, *Religion and the Northern Ireland Problem*, Dublin: Gill and Macmillan, 1984, p. 66.
54. Ibid.
55. MacEoin, op. cit., p. 225.

5
DIRECT RULE

The Ulster Catholics greeted the end of Stormont with joy and jubilation, but for the Protestants it was a stunning shock. An air of doom predominated as the Ulster Cabinet met for the last time, and there was much bitterness against the policy of the British government. Edward Heath, the British Prime Minister, was compared with Hitler, and there was a common consensus that this was the way in which 'Britain placates its enemies and crucifies its friends'.[1] Thousands of people had gathered at Stormont to hear what had brought about the final downfall of their Parliament. Fortunately Paisley was not present to whip them into a fury, and they dispersed sadly and quietly with the fear of British betrayal more firmly embedded in their minds.

Stormont had contained within itself the seeds of its own destruction. Even a sympathetic biographer of James Craig (Northern Ireland's first Premier) and admirer of his calmness, determination and courage has admitted that he failed from the beginning to encourage the minority to participate in the Province's political and social affairs. Perhaps the greatest defect was the abolition of that safeguard for the minority — Proportional Representation (P.R.) — which had been built into the original Stormont constitution. Thus in 1922 Craig agreed to the abolition of P.R. in local elections, and in 1929 saw that it was done away with in parliamentary elections.[2] He had disliked from the start Westminster's insistence that elections in Northern Ireland should be on that basis. The general election of 21 May 1921 was the only one in United Kingdom history hitherto to have been held even partly by P.R. Now, however, as direct rule from Westminster came into force, the Catholics looked forward to a better dispensation, and it cannot be doubted that the British government intended that justice would be done.

A survey of the events of the post-Stormont period up to the present certainly indicates that there is no single and final solution to the problem of a divided Ulster, but it also reveals that the attitudes of the Ulster Protestants have changed in certain ways which would have been inconceivable in the early years of partition. The first of these events was the experiment of power-sharing. The Westminster government's White Paper of 1973 announced the creation of an elected Assembly of seventy-eight members for Northern Ireland with a power-sharing Executive. It aimed at satisfying three parties: the Catholics, who would have seats; the Protestants, who would be guaranteed the constitutional position of Ulster within the United Kingdom; and the Republic, which would play a part with the resurrection of the long-dormant concept of a Council of Ireland to promote more fruitful contacts between Ulster and the Republic. Agreement was reached to the effect that there would be an Executive of which six members would be Unionists, four S.D.L.P. members, and one from the Alliance. It would be headed by Brian Faulkner, now showing how flexible a hardline Protestant could be, with the moderate Catholic S.D.L.P. leader Gerry Fitt as his deputy. This was warmly endorsed by the Prime Minister of the Irish Republic, Liam Cosgrave. Internment was to end, and a Council of Ireland would be set up. A conference at Sunningdale near London would meet in December 1973 to work out all the details.

As a result of this conference, where the Irish government solemnly declared that 'there would be no change in the status of Northern Ireland until a majority of the people of Northern Ireland desired a change in that status', it might have been thought that the majority of Ulster Protestants would have been glad to welcome the experiment of power-sharing. But in January 1974 the Ulster Unionist Council rejected the Sunningdale agreement, and Brian Faulkner resigned as its leader. The Unionists were afraid that the South was not genuinely committed to the pledge it had made regarding the position of Northern Ireland — for, as was pointed out in the Dail by Kevin Boland of the Aontacht Eireann Party, such a pledge ran counter to the existing constitution of the Irish Republic (Articles 2 and 3). Despite dismissal by the Irish High Court and Supreme Court of an action subsequently taken by Boland, the Unionists of Ulster were not placated, and Ian Paisley had to be forcibly removed from the Northern Ireland Assembly.[3]

Various reasons have been given for the failure of the Sunningdale agreement, such as the Unionists being confirmed in their fears by a statement about the unification of Ireland made by Liam Cosgrave in a television interview in the Republic, and the failure of Harold Wilson, who had defeated Heath and was again the British Prime Minister, to break the general strike called by the Ulster Workers' Council. The Council had strong support from Protestant trade unionists, and its action effectively paralysed the industrial and commercial life of the province. But at the end of the day it was the uncompromising attitude of the Protestants. Clinging to their traditions and belief that Stormont could be restored, the Unionist Council proved, as Brian Faulkner said, that it was 'an archaic body designed for a situation which no longer existed'.[4] However, an opinion poll taken at the time showed that while 78 per cent of Catholics strongly favoured power-sharing, only 28 per cent of Protestants were for it.[5] It remained to be seen if new initiatives by the British government could induce other Unionists to change their attitude and adopt the way of compromise rather than confrontation. But although in its five months of life the power-sharing Executive had shown that the Catholics and Protestants could plan and work together, the hardline Protestant leaders were doing everything in their power to prevent such initiatives. Thus Paisley, William Craig and Harry West formed the new United Ulster Unionist Council. Their activity, plus the Workers' Council strike, merited the accusation of Harold Wilson that they were 'sponging' on the British taxpayer, on Westminster and on British democracy. He asked: 'Who do these people think they are?' The reply, 'We are Loyalists!', must have sounded very 'Irish', and because the extremists on the Protestant side keep on reiterating this reply to a bemused English public, we should try at this point to understand what it is that they mean by it.

In the Presbyterian tradition in Ulster, as we have seen, there has been from the beginning anti-establishment feeling, political radicalism, intransigence and rebellion.[6] This was true at the siege of Derry in 1689, because James II was the legitimate King of Ireland, and in resisting him the defenders of the city were involved in an act of rebellion, with full acceptance of the possible consequences.[7] For them the meaning of 'loyal' was 'lawful', and this law took the form of a strict covenant or bond between sovereign and subject, which placed a mutual obligation on each — 'the King to protection and just government, the subject to pay tribute and due obedience'.[8] The thinking of Ulster Protestants is still determined by such covenanting and social contractual theories, so that they maintain that 'citizens owe only conditional allegiance to the government and that rebellion is perfectly justifiable should the government be deemed to be failing in its duty towards its citizens or any group of them.'[9] Thus James Craig was quite serious and not bluffing when he contemplated a rebellion against the third Home Rule Bill. In that tradition, Ian Paisley says: 'We hold no allegiance whatsoever to the Wilsons and Heaths of this world. Our fathers rejected the attempts of the British parliament, swayed by Irish Nationalists, to force home rule on Ireland. If the Crown in Parliament decreed to put Ulster into a United Ireland we would be disloyal to Her Majesty if we did not resist such a surrender to our enemies.'[10] Probably Paisley would justify riots by using the words of the Reverend Hugh Hanna ('Roaring Hanna' to the locals), a

Presbyterian minister who was involved in many riots in 1857. Asked whether he would preach when he knew a riot would take place as the result, Hanna said: 'I would, sir. Our most valuable rights have been obtained by conflict, and we cannot maintain them without that. We must submit to the necessity.'[11]

Ulster people's loyalty, therefore, is conditional. If Westminster does not keep its part of the bargain to maintain them in the United Kingdom, then they think they have the right to rebel. Indeed, according to the logic of Paisley, they would be disloyal if they did not. Statements by the Unionist Party leader Harry West, and by the Reverend Martin Smyth, Grand Master of the Orange Order, confirm this view of loyalty. Mr West says: 'While we proclaim loyalty to the British Crown we do not necessarily follow the dictates of any British political party at Westminster.' And Mr Smyth: 'Thank God our loyalty is not to any particular Westminster government but to the throne, which is above squalid party politics.'[12] According to this view of loyalty — the view of Paisley, William Craig, Harry West and the various forms of Unionism they represent — Ulster people alone have the right to determine how Ulster should be governed, and to oppose or reject policies or institutions created by Westminster. It was on this basis that they opposed Brian Faulkner and his new Unionist Party of Northern Ireland (U.P.N.I.) for accepting the power-sharing concept of Westminster under the Sunningdale agreement. As Richard Rose points out, Article 2 of the U.P.N.I. constitution endorsed 'the principle of agreed coalition' and 'democratic participation by all sections of the community'. But this attempt at consensus was not the policy of Stormont, nor does it fit into the traditional Unionist view.

The position of the Loyalists rests upon the basic principle enunciated by James Craig, Lord Craigavon: a Protestant parliament for a Protestant people. If Westminster departs from this principle, which was the foundation-stone of Stormont, and tries to bring Catholic members into the Cabinet through the concept of power-sharing, then the Loyalists insist that they have the right to break the laws which are enforced by such an Executive. Such laws are illegitimate and those who refuse to comply with them are not lawbreakers at all but ultra-loyal. Paisley expresses this point when he says:

'It is a process of democracy to change laws that are bad. Are all laws infallible?. . . It is wrong to say that because a law has been made it is a good law. . . This Parliament [Stormont] came into being and . . . the Unionist Party came to power as a result of resisting the law, defying the police, arming the community and declaring that the Westminster Government's proposal to put us out of the United Kingdom was not acceptable. Let no member of the Government party tell us that the law must never be broken; their whole history rests on an effectual defiance of Westminster's laws.'[13]

Such a view of loyalty grants a licence to paramilitary organisations and confirms the proposition that Paisley is indirectly responsible for much of the civil strife in the North of Ireland. But the failure to understand this traditional Ulster definition of loyalty makes mainland British people treat the trouble in the province as irrational and incomprehensible. People there, they feel, are not behaving in a British way and are bitter and bigoted religious fanatics. 'While these traits have been manifested by the extremists in their blocking of Westminster initiatives, it is certainly not true of many Ulster Protestants who are decent Christians, neighbourly, advocates of liberty, often bewildered and embittered by what appears ill-informed, self-serving attacks by their co-religionists.'[14]

Is this 'loyal rebel' capable of changing? It happened with Brian Faulkner, but could it happen with Paisley and William Craig? Could it happen to the ordinary worker tired of the bombing, conflict and carnage? When we consider the events of the period of direct rule from the abolition of Stormont up to the time of writing, the answer seems rather negative. A second initiative by Westminster — the Constitutional Convention in July 1974 — never got off the ground because of the Loyalists' obstruction tactics. The violence continued with U.D.A. assassination squads, the destruction wrought by the Provisional I.R.A., the murder of Lord Mountbatten and members of his family, the massacre of a group of British soldiers and ... The list of atrocities was endless, and any hope of a solution or a change in people's minds appeared illusory.

But there was a positive side; rays of hope could be discovered in the darkness of suffering. Evidence showed that the hardliners might be willing to compromise. Even Paisley appeared to show signs of a willingness to change. He had secret talks with the moderate Catholic S.D.L.P., and it appears that he reached some agreement with them regarding social policy. Again, his links with the Orange Order appeared tenuous, and he was never in genuine accord with the Reverend Martin Smyth, the Grand Master. With the S.D.L.P. he opposed the introduction of internment 'in principle', and he was against the Criminal Justice (Temporary Provisions) Northern Ireland Act of 1970, which provided a minimum mandatory prison sentence for anyone convicted of 'riotous behaviour', disorderly behaviour or behaviour likely to cause a breach of the peace. It was proposed that these minor charges should incur a prison sentence of six months instead of a fine, and it was to Paisley's credit that he opposed the Act.[15]

Even more significant was a radio interview which he gave in the Irish Republic. Asked if he saw himself as the Prime Minister of Northern Ireland, he appeared delighted at the prospect and talked about co-operation with the South. He said that if Protestants could be sure that the Catholic Church would no longer dictate policy to the Dublin government, and if the theocratic nature of the 1937 Free State Constitution were altered, 'then there would be a new set of circumstances where there could be neighbourliness in the highest possible sense, and in those circumstances there would be a situation different from any that existed when the country was divided.'[16] At this there was a howl of protest from his hardline followers, and Paisley quickly withdrew to his usual position. He could not afford to lose their support, since it had been by playing on their fears of a united Ireland that he was able to rise to power. Nevertheless, a view of Paisley that concentrates only on his blocking of Westminster initiatives such as the Constitutional Convention in August 1975, his attempt to start a second workers' strike in May 1977, and his opposition to the Anglo-Irish (Hillsborough) Accord of 1985, and fails to notice these signs of flexibility, is not an entirely true one. How far he can bring about changes in his followers, under pressure from crisis situations, without losing their support may be the factor which determines his involvement in the compromise that Westminster sees as the answer to most of Northern Ireland's problems. It may be that the task will not be too difficult because, as we shall shortly see, changes in traditional attitudes have taken place at the grassroots level.

But for the moment we need to think of another hardliner, William Craig. At first glance he appeared the most inflexible. He founded the Vanguard Unionist Party (V.U.P.) in March 1973 as a breakaway from Brian Faulkner's Unionist Party; this followed on from the founding in February 1972 of the Ulster Vanguard, which organised protests against Westminster initiatives. These Unionists advocated the possibility of an independent Ulster, despite their preference for staying in the United Kingdom. They also kept in close touch with paramilitary groups — and with trade union shop stewards, in order to be able to use the 'strike weapon' for political ends. Craig expressed regret at such actions, but argued that they were justifiable in order to defend the rights of Ulster. But at times even he showed signs of a more mellow attitude, as during the Northern Ireland Convention proposals when he appeared willing to accept power-sharing or some form of coalition. This was more in accord with his professional training as a lawyer and his undoubted cosmopolitan outlook.[17] The incident occurred on 26 August 1975, when the three Loyalist groups, led respectively by Craig, Paisley and West (V.U.P., D.U.P., U.P.), put forward a negotiating document. They had come together under the umbrella title United Ulster Unionist Council, and proposed for the S.D.L.P. the prospect of a voluntary coalition in the light of the crisis situation in Northern Ireland. This would operate in the Convention proposed in the White Paper of July 1974, which had been put forward after the failure of the power-sharing Executive. Craig took the initiative, but ran into difficulty with his Loyalist colleagues over the final clause in the U.U.U.C.-endorsed document of 26 August, which accepted a coalition government on a voluntary basis in times of crisis. Craig argued that because an emergency coalition would be based on voluntary consent, which could be withdrawn by the Loyalist majority as and when it wished, it would not be compulsory power-sharing.[18]

Craig did not seem as worried as the other Unionists about the S.D.L.P.'s desire for a Council of Ireland, but they were concerned too about his aspirations to be the chief political figure in such an emergency coalition. They were not convinced by his arguments — which were quite sound — that an emergency coalition was not compulsory power-sharing. In general the hardliners could not accept Craig's urging that positions in Cabinet be given to Republicans. In the event he was expelled from the U.U.U.C., but it is significant that some paramilitary groups supported his stand.[19] The support for Craig showed that there was a growing change of outlook among hardline Protestant people, and this was demonstrated in the most unlikely quarter: the Ulster Defence Association (U.D.A.). The largest of the Protestant paramilitary groups, it had been involved in violence and sectarian killing since 1969, but surprisingly had managed not to be declared illegal. A growing mistrust of the intentions of Westminster and a belief that Unionist politicians were not representing their true interests drove them to initiate talks with the S.D.L.P., the Dublin government and the Provisional I.R.A. Disenchanted with Britain, they formed the new bizarrely-named Ulster Political Research Group and turned to the United States for help.

The purpose of the U.D.A. was to found an independent Ulster free from both the United Kingdom and the Irish Republic. In 1978, at a meeting with a group of United States Congressmen who were visiting the province on a fact-finding tour, they explained that they were reacting against Loyalist politicians who did not represent their feelings and had tried to manipulate the hopes and fears of the working people for their own selfish ends. Glenn Barr, one of the leaders, argued that the new Ulster would be based on the United States Constitution and provide for a presidential democracy with a bill of rights to protect the minority.

Barr rejected power-sharing with the Catholics, but claimed that no group would be able to control the government since a two-thirds majority would be needed to do this. He projected the idea that the United States would oversee the first twelve years of the new state to ensure that there would be no deviations from non-sectarian principles.[20] However, even though a delegation from the U.D.A. travelled to the United States in January 1979 to reinforce the proposal, this 'pipe-dream' failed to impress the Americans who — as the whole affair demonstrated — were not going to be as easily influenced by flag-waving Unionist politicians as before the troubles.

However, from the I.R.A. side there was also an apparently sincere effort for peace. This centred around the political proposals of David O'Connell, one of the leaders of the Provisionals. He envisaged a federal state for Ireland consisting of Ulster, Munster, Leinster and Connaught, which would be under the control of the Dublin government. He held out an 'olive branch' to the Ulster Protestants, promising that they would not be swamped in such a federation. Ulster needed to shake itself free from British control and initiatives. O'Connell entered into discussions with the Loyalists, and used Protestant clergymen as a contact with the British government. His strategy led to a number of ceasefires, one of which lasted for six months in 1975, and forced the British to end internment and stop holding suspects without trial. One can only speculate as to how far O'Connell might have succeeded with his peace initiatives had he not been arrested by the Irish police in 1975. Jack Holland points out that there was 'no one of any political stature in the movement who could take his place'.[21]

Another hopeful sign of change in traditional attitudes was the Peace Movement. This was started by women who were weary of violence in the streets of Belfast. Catholic and Protestant women paraded singing, praying and calling for peace. The world media immediately took up their challenge and beamed their message far and wide. Here was another example of how the Ulster people could work together and seek

Direct Rule

to end the divisions which so many of their leaders, both political and ecclesiastical, had created.

Their message was inspiring:

We have a simple message for the world from the movement of peace.
We want to live and build a just and peaceful society.
We want for our children and for ourselves, our lives at home, at work and at play, to be lives of joy and peace.
We recognise that to build such a life demands of us dedication, hard work and courage.
We recognise that there are many problems in our society which are a source of conflict and violence.
We recognise that every bullet fired and every exploding bomb makes that work more difficult.
We reject the use of the bomb and bullet and all the means of violence.
We dedicate ourselves to working with our neighbour, near and far, day in and day out, to build that peaceful society in which the tragedies we have known are a bad memory and a continuous warning.

Praise and support poured in from all sides, culminating in the award of the Nobel Peace Prize in 1977 to its leaders Betty Williams and Mairead Corrigan.

Why, then, did it ultimately fail, when there was such desire for peace in the province and much backing from world opinion? Certainly, it raised questions which were not resolved. Was this 'people power' communistic? Would it become like the Civil Rights movement? Was it seeking peace without radical change? Was there too little Protestant involvement? Did it suffer from financial needs that were not being met, and did it lack a political strategy? Did the two young women who were its leaders come under too much pressure?

In Lord Longford's eyes the movement was too middle-class, without appeal to the workers. His story of an incident on the (Protestant) Shankill Road in Belfast crystallises this argument. A group of women were forming a human barricade to stop a bus burning. Reporters arrived, and asked the women if they had the backing of Betty Williams and Mairead Corrigan, both of whom were Catholics. 'We are Shankill peace women,' came the instant reply, 'We don't want Fenians up here.' 'Fenian', as we have noted, is the Loyalist term of abuse for Catholics.[23] The basic reason why the movement failed was that while many in Northern Ireland desire peace and willingly enter such an enterprise, they cannot break free from traditional bigotry. They want peace but only on their own terms.

However, the Churches continued the search for peace during the period with some degree of success. They welcomed the various initiatives of the British government, and groups of clergy held meetings with the I.R.A. Catholic priests and Protestant ministers condemned the violence of both the U.D.A. and the I.R.A., and the Protestant Churches insisted that they were not committed to the Unionist Party or the Orange Order. A League of Prayer and Reconciliation was launched in 1972, and united religious services of Catholics and Protestants were held in various places.[24] However, the Catholic Church, by officiating at I.R.A. funerals, appeared to the Protestants to support terrorism. At the same time, Protestant Churches conducted funerals for U.D.A. and U.V.F. members. From time to time Catholic churches were attacked and vandalised, and at a peace conference between Catholic and Protestant clergy held at Ballymascanlon, Dundalk, in 1973, Ian Paisley as usual led a demonstration of protest. But the Catholic Bishop of Derry, Edward Daly, did condemn the I.R.A., saying that it was 'of the devil', and underlined the futility of a military victory. On the other hand, Protestant ministers had little to say about the workers' strike that ended power-sharing.[25]

Perhaps the most serious attempt by the Churches consisted of the meetings with I.R.A. representatives in December 1974. This demanded great courage and determination on the part of the Protestant clergy, and they measured up to the occasion. Contact was made in County Donegal at a seaside hotel and at the village of Feakle in County Clare. The clergy drew up a draft declaration that the British government might conceivably make and which would not be a betrayal of the people of Northern Ireland. Their purpose was to urge the government to make such a declaration if it would in fact enable the Provisionals to declare a ceasefire. It ran as follows:

1. H.M. Government solemnly re-affirms that it has no political or territorial interests in Northern Ireland beyond its obligations to the citizens of Northern Ireland.
2. The prime concerns of H.M. Government are the achievement of peace and the promotion of such understanding between the various sections in Northern Ireland as will guarantee to all its people a full participation in the life of the community, whatever be the relationship of the Province to the E.E.C., the United Kingdom or the Republic of Ireland.
3. Contingent upon the maintenance of a declared ceasefire and upon effective policing, H.M. Government will relieve the Army as quickly as possible of its internal security duties.

4. Until agreements about the future government of Northern Ireland have been freely negotiated, accepted and guaranteed, H.M. Government intends to retain the presence of armed forces in Northern Ireland.
5. H.M. Government recognises the obligation and right of all those who have political aims to pursue them through the democratic process.[26]

Those members of the Provisionals who were present at Feakle reacted favourably to the draft proposal, but when they discussed it with their Army Council the reaction was not so good. However, the Army Council did agree to an eleven-day ceasefire with the understanding that this might be extended. The clergy duly pursued their objective at Downing Street on 1 January 1975, and the I.R.A. extended the ceasefire till 16 January. However, the government said that there would be no major changes in interment policies unless the ceasefire were further extended. It also rejected all proposals for talks with the I.R.A., either through intermediaries or directly.

Merlyn Rees, who was then Northern Ireland Secretary in the British government, thus missed a good opportunity. Such a time of ceasefire has occurred rarely, and provides the best occasion for talks. Rees may have realised his mistake, for as Gallaher and Worrall point out, he authorised shortly afterwards (15 January) meetings between two of his aides and representatives of Provisional Sinn Fein. 'No explanation of this apparent volte-face was ever forthcoming, and it seemed strange that talks which had been refused in the circumstances of ceasefire could take place while hostilities were nominally in progress.'[27]

Paisley, however, remained the dominant figure and topped the poll in the election for the European Parliament, with Northern Ireland voting as a large constituency. He claimed that he was now able to speak for Ulster Protestants, and successfully opposed a plan for Pope John Paul II to visit the province when he visited the Republic in 1979. His shadow also hung over ecumenical discussions, although these continued in the 1970s with a remarkable degree of friendliness and cordiality. But, whether due to Paisley's protests or the fear of his exploiting the fears of their conservative congregations, or the World Council of Churches giving grants to the Zimbabwe Patriotic Front, whose guerrillas were guilty of the murder of missionaries — or a mixture of all these factors —, the Presbyterian Church Assembly decided to withdraw from the World Council in 1979.

On the vexed question of separate education, the Churches had a wonderful opportunity, when an Act was passed at Westminster on

25 May 1978, to facilitate the establishment of schools likely to be attended by pupils of different religious affiliations or cultural traditions, but it was not put into general operation. The Catholics argued that separate education did not lead to civil strife, and that their schools were essential for the survival of the Catholic faith, but there were some dissenting voices. The Protestants favoured integration, but some denominations such as the Church of Ireland feared losing the denominational schools they still retained in the Republic.[28]

Amid all these events of the 1970s and early 1980s — Darlington (recognition of the 'Irish dimension', control of security by Westminster, civil rights for all, a new Executive responsible to a single-chamber Assembly) in September 1972, Sunningdale (a reformed political Assembly for Northern Ireland and the Council of Ireland) in December 1973, the Constitutional Convention in 1975 to consider how the political majority and minority could participate in government, the 'H-Block' hunger strikes, negotiations with the I.R.A., the Peace Movement, and so on — British peacemakers, in the shape of Northern Ireland Secretaries, came and went: William Whitelaw (locals called him 'Willie Whitewash'), full of diplomacy and exuding confidence and goodwill; Francis Pym, who appeared at times to be out of his depth; Merlyn Rees, whose frowning face masked a thoughtful concern; Roy Mason, effective, tough and forceful. . . . All must have been bemused by the proliferation of political parties in Ulster and the various proposals: Vanguard, nursing the sense of betrayal by the British and at times contending for a Unilateral Declaration of Independence; the Democratic Unionists, vacillating between total integration with the United Kingdom (though aware that the mainland did not want them) and the reinstatement of Stormont; and the S.D.L.P., arguing for power-sharing and an Irish dimension. But the Orange Order left no doubt as to its position; as ever, it stood firm for the cherished citizenship in the United Kingdom and the constitution. In a second Ulster Covenant signed by 334,000 Ulster people, it affirmed that 'in the event of the constitution of Northern Ireland being suspended or abnegated against the will of the people, freely and democratically expressed for half a century, we further solemnly pledge ourselves to work unremittingly for its complete restoration without tie or bond.'[29]

How far is the Ulster Protestant fear of betrayal by London legitimate? Despite assurances over the years from Westminster, Orange fears as expressed above continued. Their justification lies in the fact that no British parliament can bind its successors. 'Thus, even if the Parliament of Northern Ireland is viewed as having, in effect, a veto power over any effort to eject Northern Ireland from the Commonwealth and to dissolve the British tie, Westminster, since it has the right to make or unmake any law whatever, could repeal the 1949 Act and — assuming the Union with Ireland Act 1800 and the 1920 Act were also repealed — transfer sovereignty over the province to Eire. . . .'[30] Even the wishes of the majority in Ulster might not be respected since, as a member of the United Kingdom, it is bound to accept the decisions and sovereignty of Westminster. Direct Rule has increased the state of fear in Ulster, which now has no parliament of its own, and the way is technically open for Westminster to undo the compromise of 1920 and make a final settlement with the Republic.[31] It is therefore in the interest of the Loyalists to end Direct Rule as quickly as possible, for currently London 'holds all the cards' and can determine Ulster's destiny.

And how far is the Ulster fear regarding the South legitimate? The Republic is seen as wanting not only to take over the province but as supporting the I.R.A. campaign to bring this about. Some writers have asserted that the average Southerner does not want the North. Thus Bowyer Bell wrote in 1976: 'The prospect of a united Ireland with one million angry violent Protestants and half that number of violent and radicalised Catholics holds little charm for the comfortable in Dublin. No one wants a united Ireland but the I.R.A.'[32] Surveys, surprisingly, show that the Southerners prefer the English to the Northern Irish, the Welsh and the Scottish, and while 68 per cent favour a united Ireland in the form of either a federal arrangement or a one-government state, 51 per cent are against paying heavier taxes to support this![33] Unification would mean cuts in living standards for both communities, and it is traumatic for those in Ulster who envisage independence from Britain when they realise that what is collected in taxes in the province is equal to about half its expenditure. Hence Harold Wilson's comment about 'sponging on the British taxpayer'.

Yet there is a territorial claim to Northern Ireland in the Irish Constitution, and there can be little doubt that successive governments in the Republic have wanted unification. The accusation of the Ulster Protestants is that the Republic has supported the I.R.A. in trying to bring down the Ulster state. In reply to the accusation, the Dublin government points to the fact that it has interned I.R.A. members, brought charges against ministers close to the Taoiseach who were alleged to have been involved in gun-running, prohibited arms shipments to Northern Catholics, patrolled its border with the North, arrested Sean MacStiofain when he was leader of the Provisionals, and generally behaved in a legally impeccable manner.[34] But the Ulster Protestants reply that many of the Southern leaders are sons of Republican gunmen, and that the I.R.A. has a headquarters in Dublin and training camps throughout the South; and further, that the I.R.A. finds sanctuary in the South from pursuit by the British Army security forces; and that the Dublin government continually broadcasts propaganda to the North. Leaders in the Republic strengthen the will of the Northern Catholics to resist law and order, and have not arrested and imprisoned noted I.R.A. terrorists. Roger H. Hull, a United States attorney formerly with the U.S. Department of State, made a survey of the evidence for and against the Dublin and Ulster cases, and stated that while Dublin is not responsible for the troubles of the North, it 'has fanned the flames of uncivil strife by financing and training Northern rebels, by urging the peoples of the North to resist the legal government authorities of Northern Ireland, and by omitting to take the requisite action to curb the effectiveness of the I.R.A.'[35]

However, there is another trait in the Ulster Protestants which, since the founding of Stormont, has made them forget the Presbyterian emphasis on equality for all: the feeling of superiority over the Catholics. They may argue that the Northern Catholics deserved unequal treatment because they were disloyal to Britain and wanted to unite with the South, but the discrimination against them in jobs, housing, votes and other areas of life was designed to keep them 'in their place'. Thus the shock when education, which received better treatment from the state, enabled middle-class Catholics to bid for jobs that usually went to Protestants, and produced the leaders of the Civil Rights Movement. Then followed the dismay at the loss of Stormont and the prospect of power-sharing under Direct Rule, which meant Catholics sitting at the highest level and making decisions that would affect the place and power of the Protestants. The Ulster Protestants see themselves as British, loyal to the Crown, and fighting on Britain's side in its wars. They are proud that their country produced such outstanding military leaders as Field-Marshals Alexander, Montgomery, Dill, Alanbrooke and Templer. They are sure that they are different from the Southern Catholics, whose disloyalty extended to remaining neutral in the war when Britain was fighting for its life. In no way will they give in to an organisation like the

I.R.A., which seeks to bomb them into a Republic that is so different from them in religion, culture, language and way of life.

Surveys made before the troubles showed that, even then, only a minority of Ulster Catholics (15 per cent) identified with Britain, while the great majority of them said they were Irish. Protestants, on the other hand, identified themselves first with Britain, then with Ulster, and only finally with Ireland.[36] In 1977 Protestants described Catholics as Irish, called them 'ordinary people', and used derogatory terms and phrases like 'priest-ridden', 'breed like rabbits', 'brainwashed', 'Republican', 'superstitious' and so on.[37] Protestants saw themselves definitely as 'power-holders', and were so described, amid other terms of abuse, by Catholics. Indeed, we may say that the Ulster Protestants see themselves as essentially superior to the Catholics, and this on the basis of religion, of national identity and of political loyalty. As for the first, they insist that their religion is true and the Catholic false; on the second they assert that they are British and therefore belong to a great community; and on the third they believe that their loyalty to the Crown and celebration of that loyalty go beyond anything that is found today on the mainland.

But this sense of superiority receives a shock when they go to England and discover that they are treated like any 'Paddy', no distinction being made between them and their Catholic counterparts; because they were born and brought up in Ireland, the English see this as meaning that they are Irish. Hence there is a crisis of identity. Indeed, they have found the Scots and Americans more amenable to their point of view: the Scots are able to recognise their descent from the Plantation, and the Americans have no difficulty in distinguishing between the Scotch-Irish and the Southern Irish. Further, the kind of Reformed Protestantism which they embrace, with its overt hostility towards the Pope and the whole Catholic faith, meets with very little sympathy on the mainland of Britain, which, in so far as is has remained consciously Christian at all, has generally moved away from sixteenth-century theological dogmatism and, through the ecumenical movement, entered into close dialogue with the Catholic Church. In the prevailing atmosphere of compromise they find themselves considered intolerant and self-righteous.

As for their future, the Ulster Protestants face a crisis. Britain's goodwill towards Northern Ireland remains, at the official level at least, and its promise to respect the wishes of the majority will undoubtedly be honoured, but Westminster requires that any Northern Ireland

Assembly be representative of the whole of the community — hence the experiment in the power-sharing Executive of 1974 and the promise in the 1974 White Paper that Britain would continue to pursue that end. It was hoped that the 1975 consultative Convention would accomplish this, but since that did not happen it has continued with the Anglo-Irish Accord made at Hillsborough in 1985.

Because this important document has caused resentment and howls of protest from Ulster Loyalists, it is necessary to look at it more closely. It was signed by Mrs Thatcher and Dr FitzGerald on 15 November 1985 at a meeting in Hillsborough Castle, the former residence of the Governors of Northern Ireland. The agreement affirmed that any change in the status of the province would only come about with the consent of the majority of the people, and recognised that the present wish of the majority there was for that status to remain unchanged. However, it established, within the framework of the Anglo-Irish Intergovernmental Council set up in 1981, an Intergovernmental Conference concerned with Northern Ireland and with the relations between the two parts of Ireland. This Conference would deal regularly with political matters, security, legal matters and the promotion of cross-border co-operation.[37]

The aim of the agreement was to promote peace and stability in Northern Ireland and help to reconcile Catholic and Protestant. This could not be done by force, but it could be done by a peaceful recognition and acceptance of each other's rights. The document proceeded to stress what is of vital importance for the loyalist — that any change in the status of the Province would only come about with the consent of the majority; but it went on to stress equally that if, in the future, a majority of the people clearly wished for and formally consented to the establishment of a united Ireland, this would be supported in the respective parliaments.[38]

Further, it was stated that the Irish government would put forward views and proposals on matters relating to Northern Ireland in so far as these were not the responsibility of a devolved administration of the province. In the conduct of the meetings at ministerial level, the British Secretary of State for Northern Ireland and an Irish minister, designated as the Permanent Irish Ministerial Representative, would take the chair jointly. It was also envisaged that other British and Irish ministers might hold or attend meetings accompanied by officials of relevant departments.

Both governments recognised that devolution could be achieved only with the co-operation of constitutional representatives of both Catholic and Protestant in the province. How this devolution might be brought about would also be the concern of the Irish government where it related to the interests of the minority community.

On political matters, no one is likely to disagree with the emphasis on protecting human rights and the prevention of discrimination, but when the document mentions electoral changes, the use of flags and emblems, and the fostering of the cultural heritage of both traditions, it treads on a thorny path. As we have seen, the cultural and religious traditions are so different that fostering them can only encourage the apartheid situation. Again, what does the Accord precisely mean in connection with flags and emblems (such as the Red Hand)? Any attempt to tamper with these, or with the processions held annually at which they are flaunted, would lead to further riots and bloodshed.

Further, the role of the Irish government is a major one, for it may, where the minority interests are concerned, put forward proposals 'for major legislation and on major policy issues'.[39] These would involve human rights, fair employment, equal opportunities and the authority of the police forces. Concerning the last of these, the Conference's intention would be to develop a better relationship between the police and the minority community and to initiate action to increase the proportion of members of the minority in the Royal Ulster Constabulary. An attempt would be made to harmonise criminal law in the North and the South and make the extradition of offenders easier.

Both governments would seek to promote the recovery of those areas which have suffered in the troubles of recent years, and if devolution could not be achieved on the basis of widespread acceptance in the North, the development of economic, social and cultural links between the two parts of the country would take place within the framework of the Conference. Here we detect a certain authoritarian ring, as if to say: 'We will go ahead even if the majority in Northern Ireland desire otherwise.' In reality the intention sounds somewhat hollow, for how can such co-operation take place between North and South without the consent of an overwhelming majority of the people in the province? Perhaps this is why one of the final articles of the Accord (Article 11) states that 'at the end of three years from signature of this agreement or earlier if requested by either government, the working of the Conference shall be reviewed by the two governments to see whether any changes in the scope and nature of its activities are desirable.'[40]

The response to the agreement when it was published was predictable.

It was immediately denounced by the two main Unionist parties in the province, the Official Unionist Party and the Democratic Unionist Party. Later the Unionists resigned their seats at Westminster in order to cause by-elections, and the results plainly showed the strength of opposition to the Accord. Rallies were held in Belfast attracting crowds of more than 100,000 people, and Unionist leaders announced their intention to withdraw from key positions in the province. The purpose in every case was to make the Accord unworkable. Dissent of a different kind came from the South. Charles Haughey, leader of the opposition Fianna Fail and a former (and future) Taoiseach, attacked the agreement on 15 November as 'a very severe blow to the concept of Irish unity', and as endorsing the guarantee of the Unionist position 'in the clearest fashion forever'. It was, he said, 'a very sad day for Irish nationalism'. At Westminster one of the Treasury ministers, Ian Gow, resigned because, as he told Mrs Thatcher, he could not support the government's change of policy on Northern Ireland, 'including the involvement of a foreign power in a consultative role in the administration of the province', which would 'prolong and . . . not diminish Ulster's agony'.[41]

However, the agreement was passed both at Westminster and in the Dáil, and Northern Ireland was called upon to comply with it. A grave defect, of course, was that the people and their representatives had not been consulted, and this, as we noted in earlier chapters, is anathema to Ulster Protestants. They have always contended for democracy, even if at times they have not practised it themselves. And they will not be dictated to either by Westminster or the Dáil, as all the protests have underlined.

On the other hand, it can be argued that they were not doing much to bring about a peaceful solution to their problems, and that therefore a fresh and independent initiative was required from Westminster. That was bound to come, as was stated in the Queen's Speech of 6 November 1985: 'In Northern Ireland my government will continue to support the security forces in enforcing the law and in working for the eradication of terrorism. They will seek widely acceptable arrangements for the devolution of power. They will seek to improve further their co-operation with the government of the Irish Republic. Renewed efforts will be made to create and sustain employment, particularly by the encouragement of the private sector.'[43]

It must be said that it is extremely unlikely that peace could ever come to the province without the co-operation and help of the South in the battle against the I.R.A. Thus in this part of its proposal, the Accord is dealing with reality. But the Ulster Protestants not only resent this 'foreign interference', as they call it, but the extent of involvement by the South with their affairs. As many of them would say, it is the 'thin edge of the wedge' — an expression much favoured in warning against the slightest compromise which would lead to further concessions having to be made. Thus they prefer to proclaim the opposite: 'Not an inch!'

The English see compromise as the answer to all problems, and it remains to be seen if this will work with the Accord. Certainly it will take more than three years to see how it is working, or indeed if it is working at all. For the time being, the ultra-Loyalist endures — Paisley, for example, and the much younger Peter Robinson, who also holds a seat at Westminster — while the more moderate figures in the O'Neill mould have passed from the scene. The future lies with the youth, of course, and in this connection there is an element that often goes unnoticed: at the last count, 46 per cent of the province's primary school children were Catholic. The reality may be that if migration does not act as a check, the majority of people in the North of Ireland may eventually be Catholic. This could make the present protests of the Unionists somewhat irrelevant.

In this chapter we have seen glimmers of change in the ultra-Loyalists, but the Anglo-Irish Accord appears to have made them resume their hardline stance once more. Thus in June 1986 the Northern Ireland Assembly, which had been set up in 1982, was dissolved and the Northern Ireland Secretary, Tom King, announced that the date for elections for a new one would be left open. Westminster reiterated its commitment to the Accord, and said that the Assembly had failed in making proposals for devolution or even in monitoring the work of Northern Ireland departments. Mrs Thatcher renewed her invitation to the Unionists for talks, but they have maintained their intransigence over power-sharing and the Irish dimension.

Can the ultra-Loyalists ever change? We shall consider this question in our final chapter, especially regarding the younger element, but in the next chapter we look at another group of hardline Protestants renowned, like those of Ulster, for their intransigence: the Afrikaners of South Africa. The Loyalists of Ulster, who have joined with much of the world in condemning the Afrikaners, may find the comparison of themselves with this group disagreeable to contemplate. But much that has occurred in South Africa has a similar look to the Ulster situation; although the problem there centres on race, it also involves history (of a migration in the seventeeth century) and religion (of the fundamentalist Evangelical type), which we have found to be determining factors in both countries leading to ethnic and religious separation. This gives us a wider perspective on the Ulster scene; it could give it to the Ulster Protestants too.

REFERENCES

1. Wallace, op. cit., p. 26.
2. P. Buckland, *James Craig*, Dublin, Gill and MacMillan, 1980, p. 113.
3. Bruce Arnold, *What Kind of Country*, London: Cape, 1984, p. 113.
4. Faulkner, op. cit., p. 245.
5. Richard Rose, *Northern Ireland*, London: Macmillan, 1976, p. 31.
6. Buckland, op. cit., p. 32.
7. A. Stewart, *The Narrow Ground*, London: Faber and Faber, 1977, p. 63.
8. D.W. Miller, *Queens' Rebels*, Dublin: Gill and Macmillan, 1978, p.
9. Buckland, op. cit., p. 32.
10. Rose, op. cit., p. 40.
11. Miller, op. cit., p. 86.
12. Rose, op. cit., pp. 39, 42.
13. Paisley's speech of 25 Jan. 1972 quoted in R.H. Hull, *The Irish Triangle*, Princeton University Press, 1976, p. 77.
14. K. Heskin, *Northern Ireland: A Psychological Analysis*, Dublin: Gill and Macmillan, 1980, p. 24.
15. Simon Winchester, *Northern Ireland in Crisis*, New York: Holmes and Meier, 1974, p. 65.
16. Heskin, op. cit., p. 123.
17. Longford and McHardy, op. cit., p. 177.
18. Rose, op. cit., p. 130.
19. Ibid., pp. 130, 131.
20. T. Holland, *Too Long a Sacrifice*, New York: Dodd, Mead & Co., 1981, p. 114.
21. Ibid., p. 136.
22. E. Gallaher and S. Worrall, *Christians in Ulster*, p. 178.
23. Longford and McHardy, op. cit., p. 180.
24. Gallaher and Worrall, op. cit., pp. 75.
25. Ibid., p. 92.
26. Ibid., p. 98.
27. Ibid., p. 101.
28. Ibid., p. 167.
29. Hickey, op. cit., p. 88.
30. Hull, op. cit., p. 107: 'The Irish Triangle'.
31. Ibid., p. 117.
32. Heskin, op. cit., p. 5.
33. Ibid., pp. 8-9.
34. Hull, op. cit., pp. 148ff.

35. Ibid., p. 158.
36. Rose, op. cit., pp. 10–11.
37. Heskin, op. cit., p. 36.
38. *Kessing's Contemporary Archives*, XXXI, p. 34070.
39. Ibid., p. 34071.
40. Ibid.
41. Ibid., p. 34072.
42. Ibid.
43. Ibid., p. 34073.

6
A COMPARISON: THE AFRIKANER

Thus far we have been thinking of the Ulster Protestants in connection with their Catholic counterparts in the North and their link to Britain. At this point, we widen the frame of reference and see if a similar type of character has appeared elsewhere in the world, displaying the same attitude towards their problems.

Here we might turn to the Southern United States and consider the deep-rooted prejudices against the advancement of black people which sparked off the Civil Rights movement in the 1960s. This movement had a direct influence on the Civil Rights Association in Ulster, which even took over its freedom song 'We shall overcome'.

However, we shall briefly compare the Ulster Protestants with the Afrikaans-speaking people (Afrikaners) of South Africa. Of course, any comparison is bound to be indirect since the Republic of South Africa is a big country with a population many times more numerous than that of Ulster, and the issue there centres on race rather than religion. South Africa is unique among surviving states because racism has been established in its laws, statutes and structures — economic, social and political; in no other country in the world has it been similarly institutionalised. Nevertheless, religion was a determining factor in bringing this about, and it gave the justification which the state required. The result in both countries was similar — separate education, separate housing, separate social life — although the legislation in South Africa affecting the minute details of daily life makes it much more annoying and frustrating.

We shall see how the separation of black and white was authorised by the Dutch Reformed Church (D.R.C.), the Church of the Afrikaner; but it must not be forgotten that religion remains an essential factor of life for all the people of Africa as it does in Ulster. Thus Archbishop Desmond Tutu: '. . . I have constantly asked the question why so few independent countries in Africa have opted for communism. From the way people talk one would have assumed that the moment a country freed itself of its colonial past it would have rushed to embrace a Marxist or Leninist dispensation. But we can count on the fingers of one hand those who have openly declared themselves to be Marxist communities. Mozambique and Angola are two — but after that you really have to start looking.'[1]

Just as the Ulster Protestants celebrate every year the victory of their ancestors over the Catholic King James at the battle of the Boyne, so do the Afrikaners remember their own famous victory won in the face of overwhelming odds over the Zulus at Blood River in 1838. And they were convinced that God had given them the victory. Before the battle they had entered into a covenant with the Almighty and sworn an oath that if God gave them the victory they would forever celebrate the day as a sign of that covenant. Hence the celebration which takes place every year on December 16. The Afrikaners, in the Great Trek that preceded the battle, saw themselves as similar to the children of Israel fleeing from the Egyptians. In their case the enemy was the English who, with their relatively liberal views, had given them a hard time in the Cape and Natal, and they saw their preservation and victory over the African natives as a sign that their people had been chosen by God. The Dutch Reformed faith of the Afrikaners embraces the same Calvinistic theology that entered into the *Westminster Confession of Faith*. It lays stress on predestination: God has chosen certain people for life and ordained others to damnation. The idea of being a chosen race has occurred to many people, including the Ulster Protestants, and Cecil Rhodes certainly had this view of the British. Such a view of the purpose of God, while it can provide an assurance of salvation, tends in all spheres of life — religious, social, economic and intellectual — to give rise to a feeling of superiority. This is clearly detectable in the Ulster Protestants; William Craig, as Minister of Home Affairs in the O'Neill administration, defended Stormont against a charge of discriminating against Catholic lawyers in judicial appointments on the grounds that they were educationally and socially inferior.[2]

While the Afrikaners' rule was clearly based on legal discrimination and showed itself in the pass laws (whereby every African had to carry special identification papers) and influx control (to prevent Africans coming in great numbers to the cities), the discrimination in Ulster was invisible, but the results were similar. Thus the Protestants held the best jobs, just as the Afrikaners do in most sectors, and both were political 'power-holders'. In South Africa, as in Ulster, housing and education are separate. The Blacks, Indians, Coloureds (mixed race) and Whites all come under the Group Areas Act, living in separate areas. This is a source of grievance especially for those Blacks who are middle-class and could afford the price of houses in the White suburbs, but are forbidden by law to live there. In Ireland, after the invasion by Henry II of England in 1172, the English who settled mixed with the native Irish and gradually became 'gaelicised' in dress and speech. But the Statutes of Kilkenny were passed in 1366 to preserve English influence, and thus a barrier was set up between the two races. This prohibited English-Irish marriages, the use of Gaelic, Irish living among the English, and Irish dress, names and laws.[3] In 1534, under Henry VIII, this policy of segregation was abandoned and a policy of conciliation introduced, but the Protestant plantation in 1607, which deprived the Catholics of their land, also erected race barriers. In towns like Downpatrick and Dungannon we find streets named English Street, Irish Street and Scotch Street. Newry and Cookstown are divided, and the present Andersonstown was a Catholic village outside Belfast, as the Bogside was outside the walls of Derry. The same divisions can be observed in Belfast today with the areas round the Shankill Road (Protestant) and the Falls Road (Catholic). After the troubles began in the 1960s, entry by Catholics into the Shankill or Protestants into the Falls became highly dangerous.

We have noted how segregated education in Ulster raises the question of how the province's problems can ever be solved if the young remain forcibly separated throughout their most formative years. Although in South Africa education is separated on racial, not on religious grounds, the effect is the same as in Ulster: children of different groups grow up without really getting to know each other. At the higher level, in both countries, there is more opportunity for the different groups to study together. The South African government has created Black universities, some with excellent campuses and facilities, and more relaxation is now being seen in allowing the traditional (but non-Afrikaner) White universities — Cape Town, Rhodes and Witwatersrand — to admit students of other races. Again, as in Ulster, this opportunity of a better education, together with other state reforms, has aroused the expectation of the Blacks, and can be seen as one of the causes of the present unrest. Just as the Catholics in Ulster were frustrated by lack of job opportunities when they had the qualifications to do the jobs they could not obtain, so the Blacks react against whole classes of jobs being reserved for Whites.

The Dutch Reformed Church has given religious backing to this separation of the races. Some people assert that so great is the influence of the Church on the thinking of the state that if it had condemned apartheid the policy would have collapsed years ago. It has consistently supported the Group Areas Act, the Immorality Act and the Mixed Marriages Act, and it was the Cape Synod which said in 1932 that a

Mixed Marriages Act forbidding inter-racial unions should be placed on the statute book. As Allan Boesak points out: 'In 1934 the Federal Council of Dutch Reformed Churches took it [the 1932 resolution] over, and the next year a missionary conference held under the auspices of the Afrikaans churches accepted it. They not only accepted it, they actually sent delegation upon delegation and memorandum upon memorandum to the government. Then in 1947 the famous conference that was held in Bloemfontein under the auspices of the Dutch Reformed Church actually worked out for the first time in full detail the blueprint of the policy that would become known as apartheid.'4 Boesak also draws attention to the *Kerkbode*, the official mouthpiece of the D.R.C., which in an editorial thanked God that the Churches had been the first to see the need for racial separation and were the first to work out a policy. This was enthusiastically accepted by the National Party when it took office in 1948. The argument is that the differences of language, culture and race make separate development permissible, and in fact the ideal is the evolutionary development of a commonwealth of nations living together and in peace and mutual co-operation. Both the Old and the New Testaments, it is asserted, accept at once the unity of people and their diversity, and do not in any way seek to force them into a unity.

Like the Presbyterian Church in Ulster, the D.R.C. is no longer a member of the World Council of Churches (W.C.C.) and deplores the fact that the W.C.C. is participating more and more in political and economic affairs. It argues that the Founder of Christianity refused to become involved politically in the struggle against the Romans and advocated no programme for socio-economic reform. The D.R.C. concentrates on spiritual salvation, not deliverance from economic ills, and contends that the W.C.C. is supporting terrorism and violence. But the D.R.C. is split into three 'White Churches'. Some adhere strictly to the idea of racial separation and would support the right-wing Afrikaner, but at least one branch (the Nederduitse Gereformeerde Kerk) insists that separation can only be justified if each race gets its fair share of land, natural resources etc. so as to be able to develop its capabilities. This part of the D.R.C. is now questioning how one group (the Whites), who constitute only 20 per cent of the population, can continue to decide what is fair and just for all the rest. Furthermore, those parts of the D.R.C. which are not 'White' (the African, Coloured and Asian) have all rejected apartheid. Their existence is the result of the missionary work of the D.R.C., but if the mother-church continues to support apartheid it may soon lose its daughters. In October 1986, the D.R.C.

finally denounced apartheid as an 'unscriptural error' and thus removed any religious justification for the system. Perhaps the Churches in Ulster might gain some inspiration from this unlikely quarter, in that both the Protestant and Catholic Churches there have in various ways supported separation. In particular, as we have noted, the Catholic Church strives for a system of separate education which results in children growing up in the community who do not know one another. Although sympathy can be felt for the Catholics, who want to preserve their faith within the confines of their own controlled Church environment, a major change in such thinking would be for the benefit of the community as a whole. In many ways the future of Ulster lies with its youth, and the sooner they are educated together the greater will be the chance of peace.

The Afrikaner can change. A striking example is Dr Beyers Naudé, who had been a nationalist and a leading member of the Afrikaner Broederbond, which we will refer to again shortly. He was destined to reach the highest positions both in Church and state, but he could not with a good conscience agree with apartheid. Archbishop Tutu has said that his work in opposition to the system has made him perhaps the most striking 'symbol of hope' in his time in South Africa.[5] Both the Afrikaners and the Ulster people have a social mix and a social system which have a powerful effect on their lives and politics. Although the Afrikaner Broederbond is a secret society and the Orange Order is not, both have the same remarkably widespread influence among their own people. The Broederbond, too, is religious, believing that the Afrikaner nation was chosen by God and performs a particular calling as a nation, and that in order for it to carry through this task, its identity must be preserved. The Broederbond had a great deal to do with the overthrowing of British influence in South Africa, which had been exerted through the constitutional and Commonwealth connection; this ended with the achievement of its most cherished object, the establishment of a Republic, in 1961, and with the working out of the separation of the races. The pioneer of the apartheid system was Dr Hendrik Verwoerd (a Broederbond member), and he, with such figures as Dr D.F. Malan and Dr P.J. Meyer, was involved in the revival of the National Party, in eclipse during the long reign of J.C. Smuts. Just as Ulster politicians know that they must watch the signs emanating from the Orange Order if their careers are to proceed smoothly, so the Broederbond exercises a far-reaching influence on the politicians of South Africa.

Detention without trial has been the experience in both countries. In Ulster the Emergency Provisions Act of 1973 was followed by the Special

Powers Act the same year, and the detentions which took place during the period of Brian Faulkner's premiership excited worldwide attention. The Irish government took Britain to the European Court of Human Rights in connection with acts of brutality committed by the army. Over the years the long detention periods in South Africa, which can be arbitrarily renewed, have excited the condemnation of the whole world, especially in the case of the Black Consciousness leader, Steve Biko.

Afrikaners, like the Ulster Protestants, oppose mixed marriages. Their argument is on the ground of race, the Ulster Protestants' for reasons of religion. But the separation is the same in both cases. It is only in recent times that the Act forbidding such marriages in South Africa has been rescinded, but in Ulster, while not legally forbidden, such marriages are considered a disgrace and offence to Protestants since, according to the *Ne Temere* decree, the children are required to be brought up in the feared and hated Catholic faith. The disgrace of racial mixing has also not died out in Afrikaner culture.

It is significant too how both countries have moved towards reform and how in that process of change violence erupted. O'Neill's reform annoyed extreme loyalists and aroused the expectations of the Catholics, as seen in the Civil Rights movement, which demanded a faster pace of change. In South Africa the new dispensation of the tri-racial parliament which included Indians, Coloureds and Whites, but excluded Blacks (it is argued that they had their citizenship in the Black 'homelands' or 'bantustans'), sparked off the violence which was the weekly, almost nightly, diet of television viewers in Europe and America. As the Prime Minister, P.W. Botha, advanced his reforms and abolished the pass laws, the Mixed Marriages Act and influx control, unrest increased instead of diminishing. The African National Congress, the counterpart of the I.R.A., began the bombing not only of 'hard' military targets but 'soft' civilian ones, and as mines exploded near farms, and shoppers in supermarkets were killed, scenes reminiscent of Northern Ireland appeared on television. The National Party headed by Botha split, as the Unionists had done in Ulster, and the extreme right-wing Afrikaners, comparable to the ultra-Loyalists of Northern Ireland, emerged. These people are historically oriented, and spend much time thinking of the meaning of Blood River and about their nation's legendary fighters in the Anglo-Boer war, and the concentration camps set up by the British in which thousands of Afrikaner women and children died of disease and starvation.

The covenant that their forefathers made with God and their belief that they are members of a chosen race sustains them in their attitude to the current violence and unrest in their land. They have always had to fight for survival, and they are sure that God will give them the victory as he has done in the past. They believe that they have been betrayed by the liberal policies of P.W. Botha, for they cannot accept even the limited power-sharing that exists in the present Constitution of the Republic. They are fully convinced that the Bible teaches apartheid — the separation of the races — and that any departure from that is heresy. Thus we have people such as Dr Andries Treurnicht (a Dutch Reformed Church minister), Jaap Marais and Carel Boshoff, and the leader of the Afrikaner *Weerstandsbeweging* movement, Eugene Terre Blanche. The hardline Afrikaners, like the Ulster Protestants, reject the warning 'Adapt or die'. They hold on to what they have, and form a new extreme party when liberal tendencies begin to assert themselves. Like the Ulster Protestants, they frequently use words like 'betrayal', 'sell-out' and 'adapt *and* die'. Treurnicht is the leader of the major breakaway party in the present constellation, called the Conservative Party.

Despite Mrs Thatcher's opposition to sanctions, Afrikaners do not feel that they can trust the British. There are ample historical reasons for this attitude since it was the British who defeated and humiliated them at the beginning of the century. It is estimated that the Anglo-Boer war cost the Afrikaner population of the Transvaal and the Orange Free State 20 per cent of its number, mostly women and children. Jan Christiaan Smuts, then a young Boer general, wrote at the time: 'Our future is very dark — and God knows how dark. Perhaps it is the fate of our little race to be sacrificed on the altar of the world's ideals; perhaps we are destined to be the martyr race.'[6] The Afrikaners are also suspicious of the English-speaking population of the Republic, who they believe are willing to compromise and are too moderate. Generally, they have given their support to the new dispensation initiated by P.W. Botha, which has opted for evolutionary change rather than having revolutionary change forced upon them. It is not thought that the English-speakers will stay and fight when the crunch comes; many hold British passports and can return to Britain whereas the Afrikaners have nowhere to go. They are considered too secular and materialistic, placing excessive value on material comforts.[7] Above all they do not share the Afrikaners' values which are grounded in a transcendent belief that God has chosen and preserved them in the land and made them witnesses to the Christian faith — here they can point with pride to the missionary endeavours of the Dutch

Reformed Church and the various branches which it has founded for the country's different races.

The Afrikaners are like the Ulster Protestants in having a siege mentality. People were surprised when P.W. Botha ordered the raiding of neighbouring countries in 1986 to destroy A.N.C. bases at the very time when the Commonwealth 'Eminent Persons Group' were in the country and some hopes of peace were emerging. One explanation was that Botha had to do something to satisfy his right wing. With landmines exploding in the Transvaal and a guerrilla war building up, he realised that unless he made a move, even at that inappropriate time, the farmers would sooner or later help to vote him out of office. In the wake of the Anglo-Irish agreement, the idea of a completely independent Ulster state appears to be gaining strength, and this is because the siege mentality insists, despite the facts, that such a state could go it alone. South Africa rejected the 'Eminent Persons Group' and their findings, called a state of emergency, defied the threat of sanctions and advocated a return to the *laager* (the defensive circle of covered wagons formed by the Boers during the Great Trek when they were under attack, and into which they would all gather). Further, the right-wingers put forward the idea of a White state which, in a way that is strangely reminiscent of Ulster, would involve partition. It seems a fantastic idea, but so is the idea of an independent Ulster. In both cases those who did not favour the rule of the state would be removed. Yet Ulster would undoubtedly become involved in a civil war if Britain withdrew, and the South would ultimately have to intervene. By a strange ironic twist, the Ulster Loyalists now claim that Westminster is ruling them in defiance of the majority, because they were not consulted in advance of the Anglo-Irish Accord of 1985 — South Africa, of course, has always ruled in that way! This, say the hardliners in Ulster, is the reason why independence must now be demanded.

Fear is a characteristic of both peoples. The Afrikaners fear to lose their identity, their language, their culture, their racial identity. The Ulster Protestants fear to lose their religion, their culture, their British identity and their link with Britain. The attitude of 'No surrender' predominates. Both fought for Britain during two World Wars, and both have a feeling that Britain still owes them something: for the Ulster Protestants it is the maintaining of the link with Britain, and for the Afrikaners it is trade and a countervailing influence against the cry for sanctions. While the British do not 'hold the cards' as they do in Ulster, their culture pervades the Republic; great attention is paid to the Royal Family, and there is a feeling that Britain will be there in the possible working-out of any solution to the problem.

The Afrikaners are like the Ulster Protestants in wanting to maintain their living standards, but if they go to the lengths of isolating themselves from Europe and America, how will they be able to afford to build up their security systems? This is the Achilles' heel in their isolationist policy, for the building up of any army is expensive, and how can they increase taxes if they lose the markets for their goods? The dependence of politics on economics can be inconvenient. Both peoples live in a climate of violence. The African National Congress (A.N.C.) was once non-violent, but is now as committed to violence as the I.R.A. has always been; its spokesmen say that the time is now past when there could be any alternative to the armed struggle. Both countries maintain a heavy army presence to resist such violence. The terrorists or freedom fighters (the phraseology depending on your point of view) have bases in neighbouring countries, just as it is alleged by the Ulster Protestants that the I.R.A. has its base in the Irish Republic. Further, it is argued that a split has developed in the A.N.C. as it did in the I.R.A. — hence the hitting of 'soft' (i.e. civilian) targets in recent times, which earlier the organisation said it would never touch.

There are ways in which P.W. Botha resembles some of the leading politicians in Ulster whom we have tried to understand. Like Terence O'Neill, he initiated reforms, but then — unlike O'Neill, who resigned — he withdrew and took up a more hardline stance under pressure from his extreme right wing. In January 1986 he seemed to be opening the way for negotiations again when he spoke of apartheid being outmoded, of one citizenship, of equal treatment and opportunities and the protection of the fundamental rights of individuals as well as groups, of peace, freedom and democracy, of accommodating all the legitimate political aspirations of all South Africa's communities. Influx control and the pass laws — perhaps the biggest cause of anger among the Blacks — were abolished. The future seemed bright; glimmers of hope, such as we saw in the last chapter in Ulster, seemed to be emerging, and then six months later, with the failure of the 'Eminent Persons' mission, a state of emergency was declared to contain the violence that was expected in connection with the tenth anniversary of the rising of the Blacks of Soweto in 1976. Negotiations with the A.N.C. were ruled out, and the siege mentality took over as external sanctions appeared to loom nearer.

Like the Ulster Protestants, the Afrikaners make it clear that they will not be dictated to: reform will take place, they say, but on their terms, not those of the 'outside' world or of violent groups in their midst.

In South Africa, as in Ulster, Britain has provided the initiative in seeking to bring about the dismantling of apartheid. Having economic, cultural and personal ties (there are 800,000 people in the country who have British passports) and a massive volume of trade with South Africa, Britain wants to see a negotiated settlement. Due to its own political culture, it is fundamentally opposed to what occurred in Ulster — the keeping of one group in an inferior position by another which has all the power and privilege — although the situation in South Africa is worse since it is a minority that holds sway over the majority. Britain wants change to take place peacefully, and for that reason urges Pretoria to release Nelson Mandela (leader of the A.N.C.) and other political prisoners unconditionally, and to lift the ban on the A.N.C. and other political parties. As it had done in Ulster, Britain continued its efforts at negotiation; the Commonwealth 'Eminent Persons Group', sent to South Africa in 1986, brought with it an opportunity to end the violence, but the dialogue did not succeed. Then Sir Geoffrey Howe visited the country in his capacity as President of the European Council of Ministers to urge that national negotiations should begin, but his mission was a dismal failure and it seemed that a complete impasse had been reached. Ulster's ultra-Protestants and the right-wing Afrikaners are equally opposed to power-sharing; this, as we have seen, is the hurdle that Westminster has never been able to surmont in Ulster, the most recent failed initiative being the 1985 Anglo-Irish Accord, and any movement to include the Blacks in the government of South Africa is seen as the 'thin end of the wedge', leading eventually but inevitably to majority rule, and is likely to cause an explosion of obstructionist tactics, similar to those which have been witnessed so often in Northern Ireland.

Both peoples are rebels: the Afrikaners rebelled successfully against British domination, just as the Ulster Protestants successfully opposed Home Rule, and the right wing in South Africa now rebels against foreign interference, and has forced the liberals in the Cabinet to walk warily in any discussion of power-sharing with the Blacks. In Ulster such rebellion bases its justification on esoteric arguments concerning the covenant and the social contract, and sees Westminster breaking the law of the original bond. And both peoples are fighters, as their achievements in war amply testify, but in both countries the moderates want to see the end of separation, and to see apartheid become association. In South Africa the ultimate consequence of power-sharing is clearly seen as majority rule; and it is furthermore argued that even if there were a bill of rights for minorities (White, Indian and Coloured), a majority government could not be compelled to respect it. The Ulster Protestants fear that power-sharing is only a step on the way to a united Ireland, and they see that step as already being taken if the Anglo-Irish agreement of 1985, giving the majority in the South a say in Ulster's decision-making process, is allowed to stick.

Of course, Ulster Protestants will argue that their situation is not like that in South Africa, and that Stormont was democratic since it had a government that was elected by the majority. They are right in that the division in Ulster is between two main groups — Catholic and Protestant, or Republican and Unionist — whereas in South Africa there are at least four main race groups, and among the Blacks there are divisions between those wanting to work for reform within the present system (Chief Gatsha Buthelezi of the Zulus and his Inkatha movement), and those calling for its overthrow (the A.N.C.). But one has to ask: if discrimination took place in Ulster on its relatively small scale, what kind of inequality would the Ulster Protestants have insisted upon had they been operating on a larger scene? Given that there are such similarities in attitude between them and the Afrikaners, would the outcome have been radically different? While they are right about Stormont and the majority rule of their province, they perhaps forget that in 1920 the partition of Ireland was a compromise which those in the South accepted because of their eagerness to gain independence from England. Indeed, the South was looking to the Boundary Commission that had been set up in the belief that Ulster would be so reduced in area as to make its continued existence as an economic unit impossible. Taking Ireland as a whole, then, the Protestants are a minority, not a majority. This is the Southern argument, but accepting, as we must, the existence of Northern Ireland, it is conceded, on the evidence of the previous chapters, that this minority got a 'raw deal'. The same applies to the majority in South Africa whom a small and powerful élite have kept in an inferior position.

Many Afrikaners and Ulster Protestants are neither bigots nor uncharitable people (peaceful scenes and good relationships do not make news, and thus are seldom seen or heard of by newspaper readers and TV watchers). Many are warm, hospitable, friendly and co-operative, as those outsiders who have lived and worked with them over long periods have invariably discovered. But they have also discovered that in the matters over which feelings run deepest — politics and religion — disagreement can quickly arouse the underlying prejudice and fighting instincts. Certainly the right-wing Afrikaners and ultra-loyalist Ulster Protestants have apparently unassailable reasons for what they do and say, but in the democratic Western world they seem an anachronism. Their theology and politics have not advanced with the times, and their history, instead of being a blessing, has become a burden. The burden is likely to become heavier as time goes on.

REFERENCES

1. *Leadership*, II, 4 (Summer 1983), Johannesburg: Churchill Murray Publications, p. 82.
2. K. Heskin, *Northern Ireland: A Psychological Analysis*, Dublin: Gill and Macmillan, 1980, p.107.
3. R.H. Hull, *The Irish Triangle*, Princeton University Press, 1978, p. 16.
4. *Leadership*, vol. I, 3 (Spring 1982), p. 33.
5. Desmond Tutu, op. cit., p. 85.
6. R.J. Neuhaus, *Dispensations*, Grand Rapids: Wm. B. Eerdmans, 1986, p. 188.
7. Ibid., pp. 71ff.

7
THE WAY FORWARD

Various solutions have been put forward for resolving the Ulster problem: complete integration with Westminster, a return to Stormont, power-sharing between the Loyalist parties and the Social Democratic Labour Party (S.D.L.P.), an independent Northern Ireland, unification with the South, and so on. The best solution, on purely practical grounds, appears to be some form of power-sharing with the S.D.L.P. This party was founded in 1970 by a group of people involved in the Civil Rights movement, and its well-known leaders are Gerry Fitt and John Hume. A socialist party as its name implies, it is dedicated to Irish unity, but only if the consent of the majority of the people of Ulster can be obtained. Although it is Catholic, the party is not sectarian, and it successfully nominated two Protestants for seats in the 1975 Convention.[1] It is prepared to work with the Westminster parliament in its proposals for reform of social conditions, and it has been shown that it enjoys far greater support among the electorate than the Republicans or Nationalists. In the 1973 Assembly election, it took 22 per cent of the total vote against 3 per cent for other Catholic parties.[2]

If a way forward is to be found, it appears that the S.D.L.P. would need, as a concession, to drop its long-term objective of a united Ireland, and a concession would also have to be made on the Loyalist side to allow the S.D.L.P. to be involved in decision-making. In other words, the Westminster solution is compromise, as the Northern Ireland Constitution Act specified: 'Executive powers will not be concentrated in elected representatives from one community only.'[3] But hitherto this solution has foundered because of one of the Ulster Protestants' main characteristics: 'no compromise', or 'no surrender'. For them the past history which stressed their superiority is precious, and encourages their belief that if they compromised they would be traitors to what their forefathers held dear. This is true of both their politics and their religion. That bigotry, intolerance, narrow-mindedness, tribalism, defensiveness, sectarianism, arrogance, siege-mentality, prejudice, obstinacy, fear, sense of grievance — all spring from this captivity to the past. What is required is a change of mentality. How is this to be, at least, encouraged? One way forward is to remove the fear of the unknown from their minds: specifically, the fear of Catholics and of a united Ireland.

Here concessions are necessary on the part of the government of the Republic of Ireland. Perhaps more sympathy might be felt outside Ireland for the Ulster Protestants if it were generally realised that Article 2 of the Republic's Constitution states: 'The national territory consists of the whole island of Ireland, its islands and the territorial seas.' This claim reinforces the Ulster Protestants' fears and encourages them to think that the Republic is working secretly with Westminster to bring it about. Yet we have noted the doubts of the citizens of the Republic regarding unification with the North, and the Republic knows that its immediate interest is in preventing violence from spreading to the South, and the establishment of some sort of power-sharing in the North which would satisfy the Catholics. If violence in the North increases as a result of the 1985 Anglo-Irish Accord, Protestant paramilitaries could become more active in the South. For these and other reasons it might be helpful if a gesture of goodwill were made to the North by the South based on the precept that it is wiser to work for short-term objectives than long-term ones. Certainly it would greatly help the cause of the S.D.L.P. if it asked the government of the Republic to repudiate its claim under Articles 2 and 3, for it would establish that the S.D.L.P. was not a Republican party in the sense which that term has for Protestants.[4] In some ways it is true that if the Loyalists are captives of the past, the S.D.L.P. are captives of a long-term objective in the future: 'The repeal of Articles 2 and 3 would need to be approved by an Irish electorate in a referendum. It could be justified in Southern Ireland as merely a "form of words" leaving unaltered a long-term aspiration to unification by consent.'[5]

In any case, a united Ireland would not simply be a take over of the North by the South. It would, rather, be a new Ireland with a new constitution and a new beginning. It could mean 'a federal form of government with the North, though answerable to the new Irish government, retaining control over local problems such as agriculture, education and health'.[6] Subsidies from Britain would have to remain for the period of redevelopment, but would be gradually phased out. The Republic has already made a goodwill gesture to the Protestant Church in Ulster by removing the 'special place' of the Catholic Church in the constitution (1972). Is it too much to ask that she make this political gesture as well?

Another fear of the unknown that needs to be removed from the

Ulster Protestants is of the Catholics themselves. Separate education fuels this fear. Here the Churches are confronted with a decision. As we have seen, the argument of the Catholics is that the Church must control education in order that their faith may be preserved. Despite their protests that sectarian education has not led to conflict in other parts of the world, it is apparent that this — the fact that the children just do not know one another because they have not studied and played together — is one of the causes of the Ulster troubles. The historical and religious differences in Ulster are in some ways unique, and there is little point in comparing them with countries where the differences of religion have not led to conflict. The Catholic Church and the Protestants are faced with at least trying the experiment of mixed schooling if they are not to let the conflict continue. If the future of Athens depended on its youth, as Socrates maintained, can Ulster's future depend on it any less? There will of course be the sectarian influence of the home, versus the school, to be reckoned with, but in their teens the young people will follow more the values of their peer group than those of their parents, and if they have been educated together and made friends, there will be hope. Since the older generation are difficult to change (Paisley, for example, passed his sixtieth birthday in 1986) and children are open and receptive to fresh ideas, there needs to be a concentration on them.

It would be useful too if the teaching of religious education in school could be broadened (as happens in England) to include the study of religions other than Christianity and Judaism. A wider knowledge of how Muslims, Sikhs, Buddhists and Hindus think, worship and behave would help to minimise the divisiveness of the Christian divisions. When I was teaching in a school in Ulster, the syllabus contained no mention of these religions. The children knew about the Old Testament and the New, but had never heard of the Koran, the Gita or Sikh scripture. Ignorance even of the difference between Judaism and Christianity is illustrated by the story of the stranger who arrived in Belfast and was being discussed by a group of women. 'Is he a Catholic or Protestant?' asked one. 'He's a Jew', replied another. 'I know,' persisted the questioner, 'but is he is a Catholic Jew or a Protestant Jew?'

As we have seen, one of the problems is that the teaching of history emphasises Britain in the state schools and Ireland in the Catholics schools. An integrated school system would lead to a much more objective account of the relations between Britain and Ireland and encourage children to judge for themselves. What hope is there of this taking place? A survey conducted by the *Belfast Telegraph* in 1968, just before the present troubles, and confirmed by Rose in 1971, showed that between 60 and 70 per cent of both Catholics and Protestants favoured integrated education.[7] Further, there are historical reasons for such integration. At the beginning of the Stormont regime in 1921, non-sectarian, non-religious education was envisaged by Lord Londonderry, who as Minister of Education strongly favoured the 1923 Education Act which sought to transform education in the North by establishing a non-sectarian system.[8] And when he was a backbencher at Westminster, James Craig had put forward the same kind of ideas as Londonderry. So why did Craig seek to get amendments made to this 1923 Act to make the state schools Protestant? A flaw in politicians is their bending to pressure in order to keep their position secure. Thus the Protestant Churches and the Orange Order mounted a protest: 'In March 1925, when Londonderry was away in England, Craig met Protestant leaders and agreed to amend the 1923 act in order to preserve party unity on the eve of a crucial general election on the border.'[9] He handled the education question as he did because he had modified his own convictions under pressure from his supporters. This occurred too over the abolition of proportional representation and over maintaining a police force which was overwhelmingly Protestant.[10] Still, those hardliners today who say that it would be wrong to have mixed schooling should look more closely at what the first Prime Minister of the Province actually believed.

The support of the Churches for an integrated education system is vital. We have seen how they have helped the distressed, sought to reconcile warring groups, talked with the I.R.A. and preached peace. The Churches, however, act as the mediators — suffering mediators, for this is a vital connection between them and their Founder. This is true of the Catholic Church, which believes that it is the extension of the Incarnation, and places emphasis on the apostolic succession. Now, here are two groups of children growing up at conflict with one another and showing all the signs and strains of such bitterness. Should the Churches not mediate and seek to bring them together? Can Cardinal Conway's arguments for separate education really stand up in such a situation? Would it not be possible for all the Protestant denominations at the Assemblies, Conferences and Synods to table a resolution supporting integrated schooling? Perhaps this is the way the Churches can lead instead of always trailing behind political initiatives. There is also a corresponding need for the integration of teacher training so that Catholic and Protestant student-teachers are educated together. It is important that the future teachers feel the full force of this change as quickly as possible, otherwise they will bring their prejudices into the classrooms of any integrated school.

Education is more than book learning, however, and one of the more hopeful signs in Ulster is the number of young people who now go abroad for holidays and take jobs outside their immediate environment. Such travel is important for the future leaders of the community in both the political and ecclesiastical spheres. As we saw in the first chapter, very few students for the ministry of the Presbyterian Church take the opportunity of studying abroad. So it might be necessary, in order to broaden their minds, that all the main Churches insist on their studying and working outside the province for a year as a compulsory requirement to complete the course. Further, the Churches could do more to encourage ministers to exchange pulpits and manses with ministers in Scotland and England during some months of the long school holidays. We did this for several years during my own ministry in the province. Again, the Churches could support and encourage meetings of Catholic priests and Protestant ministers to hold regular gatherings to get to know one another better. Of course the big barrier to the last suggestion is the membership of the congregations. If James Craig was worried about his support at the 'grassroots', the minister of religion also has to walk warily. Mostly he faces people who hold firmly to traditional values, and fear, above all else, a 'sell-out' of their faith. The minister fears the loss of people to Paisley and other 'fringe' groups, and his salary is dependent on the freewill offerings of his congregation. But although he must proceed cautiously, he cannot forever avoid criticism if he is to follow in the steps of his Master. Certainly the present situation — where it is justly accused against the Ulster people not only that the Catholics and the Protestants hate one another, but that they do so 'in the name of Christ' — cannot continue.

The moderates, of course, have shown by their ecumenical dialogue that they would not be averse to such suggestions, but it is the extremists on both sides of the divide who cause the problems. Yet we have seen signs of hope in previous chapters, with even the U.D.A. talking with the I.R.A. and Ian Paisley being conciliatory provided certain concessions were made by the Irish Republic. The attitudes of the hardline Presbyterians have been under a subtle form of assault from another direction. They have to face the reality that their mother-Church of Scotland is moving away from certain sentiments in the *Westminster Confession of Faith* which they hold dear. The General Assembly of the Church of Scotland agreed in 1986 that certain clauses in the

Confession (it is the Kirk's principal subordinate standard) were 'offensive to Christians in this modern age'. Dr Kenneth Stewart, an obstetrician from Stirling who had worked with a Roman Catholic mission in Zimbabwe, told the Assembly of his astonishment at finding offensive statements about Roman Catholics when he read the *Westminster Confession* before becoming an elder. The seventeenth-century document had been written, he said, at a time of seething unrest, civil war and hatred. 'That belongs to the past,' he said. 'Times have changed. The Pope and the Roman Church have changed. So also has the Church of Scotland.' Thus the Assembly decided to disassociate itself from certain sections of the *Confession* such as the belief that the Pope is 'Anti-Christ — a man of sin and son of perdition', and that followers of the true reformed Church should avoid marrying 'infidels, Papists or other idolators'. Dr Stewart acknowledged that the preamble to ordination includes the 'liberty of opinion' Clause, but felt that the clauses he specified were beyond modification, the only remedy being their exclusion. The Assembly approved his petition by an overwhelming majority.[11] It is undeniable that problems remain for the Reformed Church over the position of the Pope, the nature of the Church, the sacraments and justification by faith, but the removal of the 'offensive' clauses at the Irish Assembly would be a step in the right direction leading to a more conciliatory attitude to the Catholic Church.

Change is also pressing upon the Ulster Protestants in regard to their identity; both their Irishness and their Britishness are being questioned. The hardliners may see the best solution to their problems as integration into Great Britain. They see great advantage in this, for it would remove at a stroke their fear of the Republic, and they would receive a greater allocation of M.P.s from the province to Westminster, which might at some time be in a position to tilt the balance of power between Labour and Conservative. But Westminster does not want this, for it would involve extra seats for Northern Ireland M.P.s and make it more difficult for the major parties to win a majority of seats. However, it is the violence since 1969 that has, in the words of Richard Rose, 'emphasised the alienness of Ulster' to the English. He points out that announcers on the British media, and British civil servants, often refer to the Ulster people as Irish. 'British politicians have no wish to end institutional anomalies and uncertainties arising from direct rule by integrating what is now often regarded as an alien part of the United Kingdom.'[12] The blunt truth is that Westminster wants nothing to do with the kind of Britishness displayed by the Loyalists, and is only held back from withdrawing the army by fear of civil war and by the promises given in the past.

In the light of this, the only course is for the moderates in Ulster to take a stronger stand against the extremists, hard though that may be in the face of intimidation and co-operate with the initiatives of Westminster. Here more encouragement should be given to the Alliance Party, which was founded in April 1970 and did its best to support the reforms of O'Neill. It does recommend continued union with Britain but draws its membership both from Catholics and Protestants. The Party stands for justice and equal treatment for all citizens, law and order, and measures against discrimination. It has nominated both Protestant and Catholic candidates for local and provincial elections, and one of its Catholic candidates, Oliver Napier, was the Alliance leader in the power-sharing executive of 1973.[13] If the Churches would make a combined move towards integrated schooling and the breakdown of social divisions this would give great support to the Alliance Party and its share of the vote would increase. The Alliance is the one political party that cuts across the divide, and its emphasis on participation by persons from both communities is consistent with what has been proposed also by the S.D.L.P.

One of the problems with both Catholics and Protestants in Northern Ireland is the length of their memories, and the storing of grievances. Whereas the English have an ability to forget and realise the blessings that come from it, Ulster people remember the past, nurse their grievances and mention them on every possible occasion. Catholics do not forget that at the time of the Plantation their land was taken from them and they were driven into the hills and bogs — or, if allowed to stay, had to serve the Protestant masters. The Protestants remember the massacres of the settlers by the Catholics and the renewed violence over the years. These events are avidly recalled when the Ulster Protestants see them depicted on the banners carried during the Twelfth of July parades, and they mourn their disasters and rejoice in their victories at one and the same time. Thus there is need for the Ulster Protestants to be constantly reminded that great nations that have fought each another bitterly in the past (Germany and Britain, the United States and Japan) are now good friends and work together for each other's good. The message can also be put in a religious context: Ulster Protestants, with their Evangelical zeal, need to remember that as God has forgiven them, so they are called upon to forgive their enemies. They need to understand too in their relations with the Catholics that if they continue to treat them as traitors, they will behave that way. Only by involving them in the political and social life of the province will they break down the mutual distrust. The idea of power-sharing and working together for the good of the country appears to be the only one offering a way forward.

In many ways they share a common religious belief with the Catholics. Both hold to the doctrine of the Trinity, the divinity of Christ, the unique value of the scriptures, and a shared ethic of opposition to such things as divorce and abortion. We have seen how the Catholic clergy insisted on an ethic which in many ways resembled the Puritanism of the North. Would the way forward not be to stress these common beliefs, rather than the difference concerning salvation which caused the split at the Reformation? Both need to realise that absolutely nothing can be gained by force. The paramilitary groups on both sides must be allowed to diminish in importance through lack of aid for their violence. These organisations could not continue on either side without support, and those who use verbal violence to stir up such terrorism must be condemned.

The attitude of the British with regard to the Ulster people needs to change too. The whole of the British involvement in Ireland, although it brought benefits, has generally been disastrous. The wars with the South, the various attempts at colonisation, the intervention of Cromwell, the punishment of Irish rebels after the 1916 uprising — these have left profound scars that the Irish have so far been unable to erase. Ulster people find that they are not differentiated from the Southerners in the mind of the English particularly, and are even made the butt of 'Irish' jokes which are designed to show that the Irish are unintelligent and illogical. Psychologically this may spring from a guilty conscience on the part of the British, but also from resentment that Ireland was the first British colony since the eighteenth century to throw off the imperial yoke. It started something which led eventually to the break-up of the British empire.

The English also convey to the Irish at times an air of superiority which is annoying both to the North and to the South. Here the protest of Ulster people at the 1985 Anglo-Irish Accord seems to have some ground. (On 30 January 1987, 400,000 — a quarter of the population — signed a petition addressed to the Queen opposing the Accord.) Even when it is admitted that Ulster politicians have not hitherto been able to arrive at a solution of their own to their problems, it does seem extraordinarily foolhardy, and to show an insensitivity to history, to impose one upon them. This is the sort of paternalism which is more and more rejected by the Africans in South Africa in face of the gradual and piecemeal concessions proposed by the Afrikaners. What we have seen in the history of the Ulster conflict is the democratic nature of decision-making that follows in the Presbyterian tradition. The Ulster Protestants erred in not extending that right to the Catholics in the past, but it would be ironic if Britain tried to do the same to them. Full consultation is required on whatever initiatives are proposed by Westminster, and perhaps the continued failure of the Anglo-Irish Accord will show this.

It may be, too, that Britain needs to change its mind concerning the continued presence of its army in Northern Ireland. It is wrong to argue that it should not have been sent in, as some writers insist, because it was a 'foreign' army. It is the army of the United Kingdom, and the Ulster people not only see themselves as British but are constitutionally part of the United Kingdom. Further, the army was only called in because of the conflict and the inability of the local security forces to deal with it. When all this has been said, however, the British army does not enjoy the confidence of the people in Ireland as a whole. This is true particularly of the Catholics in the North, who first received the army with friendship and cups of tea, but this relationship soon deteriorated as the army took a hard line with the I.R.A., to whom the Catholics have traditionally looked for protection. Since the Catholics now consider the army to be partisan, as they once did the Royal Ulster Constabulary, it might be wise for Britain to think again and propose, or accept, an international peacekeeping force. There is no guarantee that it would be more successful, but it would be immune from the general feeling of opposition to anything British, and would therefore start with an initial advantage. Further, the withdrawal of British troops would be warmly welcomed in mainland Britain. Hugh Fraser, a Conservative member of Parliament, speaking on the 1973 White Paper, asked: 'How long before we soldier out — not on? How long before we disengage? How long before we decolonise?'[14] Millions today would echo that sentiment. This would not mean that Britain can opt out of taking initiatives, which it owes to a country it has exploited in the past; and the majority of the Ulster people continue to look to Britain for the solution.

The English fail to understand the Ulster Protestants because religion is not very important for them today. They argue that religion should be kept out of politics, and did so pointedly when the Bishop of Durham, David Jenkins, spoke on behalf of the striking miners in their strike of 1984 – 5. But what if they found themselves in a similar situation to that of the Ulster Protestants? If a Catholic state such as Spain ventured to take over mainland Britain, and there was a possibility of the venture succeeding, would they not share the fears felt by the Ulster Protestants today? If the analogy appears to break down because Britain does not share the same landmass with Spain, surely it has not been altogether forgotten that Spain once sent an armada of ships to conquer the British Isles. They forget the deep differences between the Ulster Protestants and Catholic Irish which we have been considering, and the fear which the Republic of Ireland's claim on the North inspires.

To me personally the events that have taken place in Ulster since 1968 have come as a surprise and a shock. Before the troubles began, the attitudes of Protestant hardliners had a fluctuating influence. Sometimes their dogmatic and rigid views were accepted, but often the majority would tire of such a stance and rescind decisions taken under their influence. When they remarked that the hardliners 'would rather die than give in', they meant it as a joke. Most people were moderate, warm and hospitable, and anxious to do a kindness rather than harm anyone. This was true of all social classes, and was especially true in a 'notorious' Loyalist area like the Shankill Road. But the events of the succeeding years have changed many moderates into hardliners. The reforms initiated by O'Neill may have appeared too small and too slow to the young people in the Civil Rights movement, but to the older Protestants the visit of the Prime Minister of the Republic to Stormont came as a tremendous shock. Then came the violence which resulted from the Civil Rights marches and the constant bombing by the I.R.A.; the split in the Unionist Party, which had held together over the years in strong solidarity, and the resignations of Prime Ministers in quick succession; and the growth of Protestant paramilitary organisations and their constant intimidation of those less bigoted and resolute than themselves. There was also the fear of losing their Protestant faith as the ecumenical dialogue gained momentum. The fall of Stormont and the imposition of Direct Rule may have been the last straw. Their moderation ebbed away and was replaced with all the negative characteristics that have become so evident to the world.

How are they to be convinced that the times have changed, and that government of the Stormont type is gone for ever? The future appears so grim that many have given themselves up to cynicism and despair. On the other hand, the changes which have been so hard to bear present a wonderful opportunity for the people of Ulster to show the world that Christians (if that word means what it says) can live together in harmony. If the things which are held in common can be stressed instead of the message of 'No surrender', and there is a willingness to change on both sides of the divide, then I am sure that the people with whom I lived for more than thirty years have the courage and will to build a united Ulster with a government that is representative of all the people.

Since much has been said in this book about religion, especially of the Reformed faith, it would seem right and proper to give a Methodist the last word. John Wesley visited Ireland several times, and the small but influential Methodist Church there emerged as the result. Wesley did not minimise differences in worship and doctrine, as some assert, but tried to stress what was held in common. The essentials were love of God and one's neighbour, a clean heart, and the showing of faith by good works. He argued that people should recognise differences in belief and practice, and be allowed to hold what is in accordance with their consciences. Such differences may prevent an external union, but they need not prevent a union of affection. All wise people must allow others the same liberty of thinking which they desire for themselves, and will no more insist on others embracing their own opinions, than tolerate such insistence from others. The vitally necessary question is: 'Is thine heart right, as my heart is with thy heart?'

Then comes Wesley's famous statement:

If it be, give me thy hand, I do not mean, Be of my opinion. You need not: I do not expect it or desire it. Neither do I mean, I will be of your opinion. I cannot: It does not depend on my choice: I can no more think, than I can see or hear, as I will. Keep your opinion; I mine; and that as steadily as ever. You need not even endeavour to come over to me, or bring me over to you. I do not desire you to dispute those points, or to hear or speak one word concerning them. Let all opinions alone on one side and the other: Only give me thine hand. I do not mean, Embrace my modes of worship; or I will embrace yours. This also is a thing which does not depend either on your choice or mine. We must act as each is fully persuaded in his own mind. Hold you fast that which you believe is most acceptable to God, and I will do the same. . . . Let all these smaller points stand aside. Let them never come into sight. If thine heart is as my heart, if thou lovest God and all mankind, I ask no more: Give me thine hand.[15]

Hands across the divide in Ulster — is there any other way?

REFERENCES

1. Richard Rose, *Northern Ireland*, London: Macmillan, 1976, p. 54.
2. Ibid.
3. Ibid.
4. Ibid., p. 149.
5. Ibid., p. 150.
6. R.H. Hull, The Irish Triangle, op. cit., p. 258.
7. K. Heskin, *Northern Ireland: A Psychological Analysis*, op. cit., p. 144.
8. Ibid., p. 143.
9. P. Buckland, *James Craig*, op. cit., p. 114.
10. Ibid., p. 81.
11. *Life and Work*, (Edinburgh), July 1986, p. 10.
12. Rose, op. cit., p. 155.
13. Ibid., pp. 58, 59.
14. G. MacEoin, *Northern Ireland: Captive of History*, op. cit., p. 288.
15. 'The Catholic Spirit' (sermon based on II Kings x.15), *Wesley's Works*, vol. V: *Sermons* (1), 1771, p. 499.

APPENDIX A
DOCUMENTS ON ULSTER'S HISTORY
Extracts and Commentary

The Act of Supremacy, 1560
The Act of Uniformity, 1560
The Plantation of Ulster, 1610
The Catholics' Demands, 1644
The Protestants' Demands, 1644
The Catholic Relief Act, 1778
The United Irishmen, 1791
Rules of the Orange Society, 1798
The Act of Union, 1800
Catholic Emancipation, 1824
The Opposition to Home Rule, 1911-14
Treaty between Great Britain and Ireland, 1925
Report of the Cameron Commission, 1969
Report of the Scarman Tribunal, 1972
Statements by I.R.A. Leaders, 1972
The Future of Northern Ireland, 1972.

Source: E. Curtis and R.B. MacDowell, *Irish Historical Documents, 1172–1922*, London: Methuen, 1943.

The Act of Supremacy, 1560

The Irish statutes relating to this Act and the Act of Uniformity, 1560, closely resemble the English ones. The Irish parliament agreed with the English demand that all clergy and officers of the Crown acknowledge the supremacy of the sovereign by taking the following oath:

I, A.B., do utterly testify and declare in my conscience that the Queen's Highness is the only supreme governor of this realm, and of all other of Her Highness's dominions and countries, as well as in all spiritual or ecclesiastical things or causes, as temporal, and that no foreign prince, person, prelate, state or potentate, hath or ought to have any jurisdiction, power, superiority, pre-eminence or authority, ecclesiastical or spiritual within this realm, and therefore I do utterly renounce and forsake all foreign jurisdictions, power, superiorities and authorities, and do promise that from henceforth I shall bear faith and true allegiance to the Queen's Highness, her heirs and successors. . . .

The Act of Uniformity, 1560

This Act called for a uniformity of common prayer and service in the Church and in the administration of the sacraments. All worship was to be conducted according to the Anglican *Book of Common Prayer*. In the event of a refusal by an minister or cleric to follow this Order,

He shall lose and forfeit to the Queen's Highness, her heirs and successors, for his first offence the profits of all his spiritual benefices or promotions, coming or arising in one whole year next after his conviction, and also the person so convicted shall for the first offence suffer imprisonment for the space of six months without bail. . . . The same person shall for his second offence suffer imprisonment for the space of one whole year, and shall therefore be deprived (*ipso facto*) of all his spiritual promotions. . . .

All shall attend Church, otherwise. . . .

. . . . [they] shall forfeit for every such offence [absence] twelve pence to be levied by the churchwarden of the parish. . . .

The Plantation of Ulster, 1610

British undertakers (English and Scotch) were given land — either 2,000 acres or 1,500 or 1,000 — and were allowed to export goods from Ireland and import necessities from the mainland. An allowance was given them of timber to build homes, 'without paying anything for the same for the the space of two years'. For every 1,000 acres they would pay His Majesty five pounds, six shillings and eight pence. This would be in two stages. The undertaker was responsible for peopling his land:

Every undertaker shall within three years, . . . plant or place upon a small proportion, the number of 24 able men of the age of 18 years or upwards, being English or inland Scottish; and so rateably upon the other proportions; which numbers shall be reduced into 10 families at least, to be settled upon every small proportion. . . . Every of said undertakers shall draw their tenants to build houses for themselves and their families, not scattering, but together, near the principal house or bawn, as well for their mutual defence and strength, as for the making of villages and townships. The said undertakers, their heirs and assigns, shall have ready in the houses at all times, a convenient store of arms which may be viewed and mustered every half year according to the manner of England.

Undertakers had to take the oath of supremacy and conform in religion, and this was necessary for their tenants as well. If they thought at any time of giving portions of their land to the 'mere Irish', such lands would be immediately forfeited. Only 58,000 acres of the settled land (the counties of Armagh, Tyrone, Donegal, Fermanagh and Cavan) would be allocated to the 'natives', and they would pay for every 1,000 acres £10 13s. 4d. annually.

The Catholics' Demands, 1644

After the failure of the rebellion of 1641, the Catholics, under much oppression, eventually presented their demands to King Charles I at Oxford in 1644. They called for all acts of oppression to be repealed. Land should be handed back to its rightful owners and. . . .

. . . . that all marks of incapacity imposed upon the natives . . . to purchase or acquire leases, offices, lands, or hereditaments, be taken away by act of parliament, and the same to extend to the securing of purchases, leases, or grants already made, and that for the education of youth, an act be passed in the next parliament for the erecting of one or more inns of court, universities, free and common schools. That the offices and places of command, honour, profit and trust . . . be conferred upon Roman Catholic natives . . . in equality and indifference with your Majesty's other subjects. . . .

Becoming more courageous, their demands extended to a free parliament:

That an act shall be passed in the next parliament, declaring that the parliament of Ireland is a free parliament of itself, independent of, and not subordinate to, the parliament of England, and that the subjects of Ireland are immediately subject to your Majesty as in right of your crown, and that the members of the said parliament of Ireland, and all other subjects of Ireland are independent, and in no way to be ordered or concluded by the parliament of England, and are only to be ordered and governed within that kingdom by your Majesty and such governors as are or shall be there appointed, and by the parliament of that kingdom according to the laws of the land.

A demand is also made for the removal of the standing army in Ireland on the diplomatic grounds that it is costing too much and it is a mark of lack of trust! As a peace offering the Catholics offer 10,000 men to suppress the 'unnatural rebellion now in this kingdom'.

The Protestants' Demands, 1644

As soon as it was known that a Catholic mission was going to Oxford, a group of Protestants secured permission from the Lord Lieutenant to send over a delegation. They called for the establishment of the true Protestant religion in Ireland, that popish clergy be banished from the country since they had always been the stirrers-up of all rebellion, and that all laws against popery be continued. All Protestant churches damaged or destroyed in the rebellion should be restored and the repair bill presented to the Catholics. All persons convicted of crime should be punished forthwith and all officials of the Crown should take the oath of supremacy. Catholic lawyers who refused to do so should be restrained from practising, since experience proved that they had 'been a great cause of the continued disobedience' of the people.

There was also a demand for further plantation of additional settlers on the lands of Catholics, forfeited to the Crown by their rebellion, and a good walled town built. . . .

. . . . and furnished with necessary and sufficient means of legal and just government and defence, for the better security of your Majesty's laws and rights, more especially the true Protestant religion, in times of danger, in any of which towns no papist may be permitted to dwell or inhabit.

The Catholic Relief Act, 1778

Catholics suffered from the penal laws, and in 1727 an Act was passed preventing them from voting at parliamentary elections. But in 1771 and 1774 Acts were passed mitigating the stringency of the penal laws. These Acts, in the light of 'their uniform peaceful behaviour for a long series of years', allowed the Catholics, provided they took an oath of allegiance to the King, to take, hold and enjoy any lease or leases for any term or term of years, not exceeding nine hundred and ninety-nine years. The oath taken shows the anti-Catholic bias that remained, in that they were called upon to repudiate. . . .

. . . . that the Pope of Rome, or any other foreign prince, prelate, state or potentate hath or ought to have any temporal or civil jurisdiction, power, superiority or pre-eminence, directly or indirectly, within this realm.

It was not till the Act of 1829 that Catholics could take seats in parliament without making declarations also against transubstantiation and the invocation of the saints and the sacrifice of the mass.

The United Irishmen, 1791

The societies of United Irishmen were founded in 1791 and tried to spread radical ideas. After 1795 the United Irishmen put pressure on the government through a network of secret societies organised in a military system. Their organisation is described in 1797 and grievances outlined: 'We have no national government, we are ruled by Englishmen, and the servants of Englishmen, whose object is the interest of another country, whose instrument is corruption, and whose strength is the weakness of Ireland. . . .'

What is needed is 'an equal representation of all people in parliament' instead of the English having the 'power and patronage' to 'seduce and subdue' the honesty of the Irish representatives in the legislature. The United Irishmen organisation was determined to counter the English influence and power by uniting all Irishmen of every religious persuasion. Bigotry in religion and politics must be abolished in favour of 'the equal distribution of the rights of man throughout all sects and denominations of Irishmen'.

Rules of the Orange Society, 1798

1. *'General declaration of the objectives of the Orange Institute'*

Under this heading the Orangeman must recognise that Orangeism is the defence of His Protestant Majesty and assistance of the civil and military power. In particular, honour is due to King William III, and the celebration of his victory at the battle of the Boyne is required annually.

We further declare, that we are exclusively a Protestant association, yet detesting as we do any intolerant spirit, we solemnly pledge ourselves to each other, that we will not persecute or upbraid any person on account of his religious opinion, but that we will, on the contrary, be aiding and assisting to every loyal subject of every religious description.

2. *Qualifications for membership*

These are based on the Christian religion and have already been referred to in the text (see above,. pp. 29–30).

3. *Obligations of Orangemen*

Under this heading certain obligations are set forth, including support and loyalty to the King provided he is a Protestant. There are various affirmations required of the Orangeman, *inter alia* that he is not a Catholic or a member of the United Irishmen. Included is a pledge of mutual loyalty between members:

'that we will be true to all Orangemen in all just actions, neither wronging nor seeing him wronged to our knowledge without acquainting him thereof.'

Finally, it is stressed that 'no Roman Catholic can be admitted on any account.'

(*Source*: H. Senior, *Orangeism in Ireland and Britain*, London: Routledge & Kegan Paul, 1966, pp. 298ff.)

The Act of Union, 1800

Resolutions in favour of a Union were passed by the British parliament early in 1799. At the beginning of the Irish parliamentary session of 1799, a clause in the Address referring to a Union was defeated in the Commons. But in March 1800 the Irish parliament agreed to resolutions similar to those passed by the British parliament the previous year. The Act of Union was introduced into the Irish House of Commons on 21 May 1800 and received the Royal Assent on 1 August 1800. It was to. . . .

. . . . strengthen and consolidate the connexion between the two kingdoms. . . . That it be the first article of the union of the kingdoms of Great Britain and Ireland, that the said kingdom of Great Britain and Ireland shall, upon the first day of January, which [shall be] in the year of our Lord 1801, and for ever, be united into one kingdom, by the name of 'The United Kingdom of Great Britain and Ireland'. . . . The second article [shall be] that the succession to the Imperial Crown of the said United Kingdom . . . shall continue limited and settled in the same manner as the succession to the Imperial Crown of the said Kingdoms of Great Britain and Ireland. That it be the third article of union, that the said United Kingdom be represented in one and the same parliament to be styled 'The Parliament of the United Kingdom of Great Britain and Ireland' . . . That it be the fourth article of union that four lords spiritual of Ireland, by rotation of sessions, and twenty-eight lords temporal of Ireland, elected for life by the peers of Ireland, shall be the number to sit and vote on the part of Ireland in the House of Lords of the parliament of the United Kingdom, and one hundred commoners (two for each county of Ireland, two for the city of Dublin, two for the city of Cork, one for the university of Trinity College, and one for each of the thirty-one most considerable cities, towns, and boroughs) be the number to sit and vote on the part of Ireland in the House of Commons of the parliament of the United Kingdom. . . .

Catholic Emancipation (Report of the committee appointed by the Catholic Association, 1824)

The Committee sees the need to find money for petitions regarding Catholic Emancipation to be presented to parliament, to procure legal redress for all Catholics injured by Orange violence, to

bring before the high courts of criminal justice all such magistrates as should participate in or countenance the illegal proceedings, processions etc. of the Orange faction, and to arrest . . . that career of violence, by which . . . so many Catholics have been murdered by Orangemen. . . .

The document calls for work rights, a liberal and enlightened press in Dublin, cheap publications to enable the children to learn in the schools, and finance to train priests to minister to 'their haughty and erratic neighbours' (i.e. the English!).

The Opposition to Home Rule

The text of Ulster's Solemn League and Covenant, 1912, which was signed on 28 September 1912 by 471,000 people, is given in the text. Here we note the opposition to Home Rule by the Southern Unionists in Dublin, 10 October 1911, and give some extracts from the speech made by Sir Edward Carson on 11 February 1914 regarding the position of Ulster in the House of Commons.

The Southern Unionists argued that the creation of a separate Irish parliament . . . .

'. . . . would produce most dangerous social confusion, involving a disastrous conflict of interests and classes, and a serious risk of civil war. Because such a measure would endanger the commercial relations between Ireland and Great Britain, and would cause in Ireland widespread financial distrust, followed by a complete paralysis of enterprise.'

The Southerners saw such a change as leading to a complete separation of Ireland from Britain, thus depriving them of their birthright 'by which we stand on equal ground with our fellow-countrymen of Great Britain as subjects of our King and citizens of the British empire'. And, how would the minorities in the country be protected? This could not be done by any 'statutory limitations restricting the authority of an Irish legislative assembly, or the power of an Irish executive.

Sir Edward Carson included the fears of the Southern Unionists in his speech, but was most vivid in describing the position of the Ulster Protestants:

'They are fighting for a great principle, and a great ideal. They are fighting to stay under the government which they were invited to come under, under which they have flourished and under which they are content, and to refuse to come under a government which they loathe and detest. Men do not make sacrifices or take up the attitude these men in Ulster have taken up on a question of detail or paper safeguards. I am not going to argue whether they are right or wrong in resisting. It would be useless to argue it, because they have thoroughly made up their minds, but I say this: If these men are not morally justified when they are attempted to be driven out of one government with which they are satisfied and put under another which they loathe, I do not see how resistance ever can be justified in history at all.'

He argues that there are only two ways to deal with Ulster:

'She is not a part of the community which can be bought. She will not allow herself to be sold. You must therefore either coerce her if you go on, or you must, in the long run, by showing that good government can come under the Home Rule bill, try and win her over to the case of the rest of Ireland. You probably can coerce her — though I doubt it. If you do, what will be the disastrous consequences not only to Ulster, but to this country and the Empire? Will my fellow-countryman, the leader of the Nationalist party, have gained anything? I will agree with him — I do not believe he wants to triumph any more than I do. But will he have gained anything if he takes over these people and then applies for what he used to call — at all events his party used to call — the enemies of the people to come in and coerce them into obedience? No, sir, one false step taken in relation to Ulster will, in my opinion, render for ever impossible a solution of the Irish question. I say this to my nationalist fellow-countrymen, and indeed also to the government: you have never tried to win over Ulster.

'You have never tried to understand her position. You have never alleged, and can never allege, that this bill gives her one atom of advantage. Nay, you cannot deny that it takes away many advantages that she has as a constituent part of the United Kingdom. You cannot deny that in the past she had produced the most loyal and law-abiding part of the citizens of Ireland. After all that, for these two years, every time we came before you your only answer to us — the majority of you, at all events — was to insult us, and to make little of us. I say to the leader of the Nationalist party, if you want Ulster, go and take her, or go on and win her. You have never wanted her affections; you have wanted her taxes.'

Appendix A

Text of the Agreement amending and supplementing the articles of Agreement for a Treaty between Great Britain and Ireland, signed 3 December 1925

The fear of the Ulster Protestant which we have noted in the text was somewhat calmed after partition and the forming of the Stormont parliament, and this was also allayed by the tripartite treaty of 1925, when the United Kingdom government, the Irish Free State and Northern Ireland decided to leave the border as it was:

The powers in relation to Northern Ireland which by the Government of Ireland Act, 1920, are made powers of the Council of Ireland, shall be, and are hereby transferred to, and shall become powers of the Parliament and Government of Northern Ireland; and the Governments of the Irish Free State and of Northern Ireland shall meet together as and when necessary for the purpose of considering matters of common interest arising out of or connected with the exercise and administration of the said powers.

In the light of this Treaty, it is understandable how Ulster fears are stimulated by any mention of the Council of Ireland; but protests about meetings between the governments of Northern Ireland and the Free State are misplaced, and Ulster Protestants should realise that such meetings are legitimate. However, the Free State under De Valera repudiated the tripartite agreement and laid claim to Northern Ireland. The 1937 Constitution in Article 2 plainly states that the national territory is 'the whole island of Ireland, its islands and the territorial seas'. This deepened the mistrust of Ulster Protestants. However, in July 1963 Sean Lemass, the successor of De Valera, did recognise the existence of Northern Ireland, not because it was occupied by the British army which the I.R.A. in its propaganda alleged, but because of the majority decision. Consequently, Terence O'Neill invited Sean Lemass to Belfast in 1965 with the results noted in the text of this book (pp. 69, 70 and 74).

Disturbances in Northern Ireland: Report of the Cameron Commission*
Violence and Civil Disturbances in Northern Ireland, 1969: Report of the Scarman Tribunal, 1972†

Both of these reports question the role of the police during the troubles and note that the recruitment and arming of the 'B Specials' appeared as a special threat to the Catholics.

CAMERON COMMISSION

Until very recent years, for drill and training purposes the U.S.C. [Ulster Special Constabulary] made large use of Orange Lodges and this, though it may have been necessary for reasons of economy and because of the lack of other suitable premises, tended to accentuate in the eyes of the Catholic minority the assumed partisan sectarian character of the force.

SCARMAN TRIBUNAL

It is painfully clear from the evidence adduced before us that by July 1969 the Catholic minority no longer believed that the R.U.C. [Royal Ulster Constabulary] was impartial, and that Catholic and civil rights activists were publicly asserting this loss of confidence. Understandably these resentments affected the thinking and feeling of the young and irresponsible, and induced the jeering and throwing of stones which were the small beginnings of most of the disturbances.

The report goes on to show that the police employed the wrong tactics in dealing with the Civil Rights protesters. This was due to the incorrect police thinking that the I.R.A. was behind the Civil Rights movement from the start. Implementation of the Special Powers Act of 1922 and internment added fuel to the fire. Gerrymandering — the manipulation of electoral boundaries — and discrimination in employment were also underlined by these two reports.

The Cameron Commission also had something important to say on the Civil Rights movement:

We have already commented on the presence of I.R.A. sympathisers and members within the Association and their acting as stewards on the occasions of marches or demonstrations. At the same time there is little

---

*Belfast: H. M. Stationery Office, 1969.
†Belfast: H. M. Stationery Office, 1972.

doubt that left wing extremists of the type already closely associated with the control of People's Democracy would be ready to take over, if they could, the real direction of the C.R.A. [Civil Rights Association] and divert its activities from a reformist policy to a much more radical course which would not exclude the deliberate use of force and the provocation of disorder as an instrument of policy.

Statements by I.R.A. Leaders, 1972

It is difficult at times to appreciate the difference between the Provisional and the Official I.R.A., apart from the fact that the former use more violence to further their aims. Both want the British Army to withdraw, the ending of all internment, and abolition of the Special Powers Act. The Provisionals claim that they shoot people not because they are Protestants but because they are agents of British imperialism. Thus they point out that they have shot Catholic members of the Ulster Defence Regiment (statement by Sean MacStiofain, chief of staff of the Provisional I.R.A.). Both are 'worker'-dominated movements, but the Official I.R.A. claims to be more socialistic and to have thought through this issue more than the Provisionals. Out of many statements we have chosen the following by Cathal Goulding, chief of staff of the Official I.R.A., in 1972:

'The basic difference between us and the Provos is that they believe that by uniting the Catholics North and South they can have a united Ireland. We say you can't. The middle-class Catholics in the North are just as worried about retaining their stranglehold over the people as the middle-class Protestants are. They'd all love some kind of settlement so they can get back to the business of making money. . . .'

(*Source:* Rosita Sweetman, *On our Knees*, London: Pan Books, 1972.)

The Future of Northern Ireland: A Paper for Discussion*

Various proposals on the future of Northern Ireland were put forward in this document by the Ulster Unionist Party, the Alliance Party, the Northern Ireland Labour Party, and the Social Democratic and Labour Party (S.D.L.P).

*London: H.M. Stationery Office, 1972.

Most of the parties agreed that the Special Powers Act should be replaced, or, as the Northern Ireland Labour party said, 'Anything in the nature of Special Powers legislation to be a Westminster matter. . . .' A Bill of Rights guaranteeing human rights to all citizens was envisaged by the Unionists, the Alliance and the Northern Ireland Labour Party.

Concerning government of the Province, the Unionists spoke of a Northern Ireland parliament of 100 members elected by majority vote, with an Executive of which the Cabinet should comprise a prime minister and five or six ministers, each heading a department. The proposal that at least three departments were to be chaired by Opposition members was important. The Alliance stressed the election of an Assembly by proportional representation, 'at maximum intervals of four years'. This was echoed by the Northern Ireland Labour Party and the S.D.L.P.

Regarding the 'Irish dimension', the most radical proposal was that of the S.D.L.P.:

An immediate declaration by the United Kingdom that it would be in the best interest of all sections of the communities in both islands [i.e. Great Britain and Ireland] if Ireland were to become united on terms which would be acceptable to all the people of Ireland, and that the United Kingdom will positively encourage such a development. Pending the achievement of unity, the establishment of an interim system of government for Northern Ireland under the joint sovereignty of the United Kingdom and the Irish Republic. . . . No representation for Northern Ireland in either the Westminster or Dublin Parliament. . . . Creation of a new national Senate for the whole of Ireland, with equal representation from the Dublin parliament and the Northern Ireland Assembly, the parties from each being represented according to their strength, to plan the integration of North and South and agree on an acceptable constitution.

This contrasted sharply with the other Catholic party, the Northern Ireland Labour Party, which was much more in line with the Unionist and Alliance. But since they had only one member in the Northern Ireland House of Commons and the S.D.L.P. had six members, it was the latter that represented the wishes of the Catholics.

It is significant that the Unionists, in considering the Irish dimension, put forward a proposal which strikingly resembles what has emerged in the Anglo-Irish Accord;

A tripartite Declaration, analogous to the Agreement of 1925, by the Governments in London, Dublin and Belfast affirming the right of the people of Northern Ireland to self-determination. Inter-governmental discussion about co-operation in ending terrorism in Ireland, and review of extradition arrangements or declaration of a Common Law Enforcement Area in Ireland. If such action is taken, the formation of an Irish Intergovernmental Council, with equal membership from the Northern Ireland Government and the Government of the Republic of Ireland, to discuss matters of mutual interests, particularly in the economic and social fields.

The Alliance Party also saw the formation of 'an advisory Anglo-Irish Council with representatives from Westminster, the Dail and the new Northern Ireland Assembly, and the Northern Ireland Labour Party proposed a 'Council of Ireland'.

The United Kingdom proposals were also included: 'The guarantee to the people of Northern Ireland that the status of Northern Ireland as part of the United Kingdom will not be changed without their consent is an absolute: this pledge cannot and will not be set aside.' But the wishes of the minority in Northern Ireland must also be taken into account together with the geographical unity of the island and the problems it shares with the South.

Indeed the Act of 1920 itself, which has for so many years been the foundation of Northern Ireland's constitutional status, explicitly provided means to move towards ultimate unity (with the South) on just such a basis; but the will to work this was never present. It is a matter of historical fact that this failure stemmed from decisions and actions taken, not only in Great Britain and Northern Ireland, but in the Republic of Ireland also. . . . It is therefore clearly desirable that any new arrangements for Northern Ireland should, whilst meeting the wishes of Northern Ireland and Great Britain, be so far as possible acceptable to and accepted by the Republic of Ireland.

The report went on to stress that minority interests should have a share in the exercise of executive power and equal opportunity for all citizens.

In March 1973, the Northern Ireland Constitutional Proposals White Paper was presented to parliament, and the Act passed on 18 July 1973. However, in the event the extremists in Northern Ireland made the new Executive unworkable.

APPENDIX B

THE WESTMINSTER CONFESSION OF FAITH, 1643
Extracts and Commentary

Election
Christian Liberty
The Sabbath Day
The Civil Magistrate
Marriage and Divorce
The Church

A central doctrine which, down the ages, had given nations a sense of being specially chosen is Election. This has sustained them in times of crisis, but has also given them a feeling that they are superior, both spiritually and socially, to their neighbours. It was considered by the Non-Subscribing Presbyterians to be an unfair doctrine, as we noted in the text, and a more liberal view was sought in the twentieth century by the German theologian Karl Barth. He argued that all have been elected, but it is possible that some will reject their election.

Chapter III: 'Of God's Eternal Decree'

GOD, from all eternity, did, by the most wise and holy counsel of His own will, freely, and unchangeably ordain whatsoever comes to pass: yet so, as thereby neither is God the author of sin, nor is violence offered to the will of the creatures; nor is the liberty or contingency of second causes taken away, but rather established.

II. Although God knows whatsoever may or can come to pass upon all supposed conditions, yet hath He not decreed anything because He foresaw it as future, or as that which would come to pass upon such conditions.

III. By the decree of God, for the manifestation of His glory, some men and angels are predestinated unto everlasting life; and others foreordained to everlasting death.

IV. These angels and men, thus predestinated, and foreordained, are particularly and unchangeably designed, and their number so certain and definite, that it cannot be either increased or diminished.

V. Those of mankind that are predestinated unto life, God, before the foundation of the world was laid, according to His eternal and immutable purpose, and the secret counsel and good pleasure of His will, hath chosen, in Christ, unto everlasting glory, out of His mere free grace and love, with out any foresight of faith, or good works, or perseverance in either of them, or any other thing in the creature, as conditions, or causes moving Him thereunto: and all to the praise of His glorious grace.

VI. As God hath appointed the elect unto glory, so hath He, by the eternal and most free purpose of His will, foreordained all the means thereunto. Wherefore, they who are elected, being fallen in Adam, are redeemed by Christ, are effectually called unto faith in Christ by His Spirit working in due season, are justified, adopted, sanctified, and kept by His power, through faith, unto salvation. Neither are any other redeemed by Christ, effectually called, justified, adopted, sanctified, and saved, but the elect only.

VII. The rest of mankind God was pleased, according to the unsearchable counsel of His own will, whereby He extendeth or withholdeth mercy, as He pleaseth, for the glory of His sovereign power over His creatures, to pass by; and to ordain them to dishonour and wrath for their sin, to the praise of His glorious justice.

VIII. The doctrine of this high mystery of predestination is to be handled with special prudence and care, that men, attending the will of God revealed in His Word, and yielding obedience thereunto, may, from the certainty of their effectual vocation, be assured of their eternal election. So shall this doctrine afford matter of praise, reverence, and admiration of God; and of humility, diligence, and abundant consolation to all that sincerely obey the Gospel.

Chapter XX: 'Christian Liberty'

Has the individual or the group the right to oppose the state when it is unjust? The United Irishmen thought so, but the Confession says that the 'powers that be', i.e. rulers, are ordained by God and should be obeyed.

THE liberty which Christ hath purchased for believers under the Gospel consists in their freedom from the guilt of sin, the condemning wrath of God, the curse of the moral law; and, in their being delivered from this present evil world, bondage to Satan, and dominion of sin; from the evil of afflictions, the sting of death, the victory of the grave, and everlasting damnation; as also, in their free access to God, and their yielding obedience unto Him, not out of slavish fear, but a child-like love and willing mind. All which were common also to believers under the law. But, under the new testament, the liberty of Christians is further enlarged, in their freedom from the yoke of the ceremonial law, to which the Jewish Church was subjected; and in greater boldness of access to the throne of grace, and in fuller communications of the free Spirit of God, than believers under the law did ordinarily partake of.

II. God alone is Lord of the conscience, and hath left it free from the doctrines and commandments of men, which are, in any thing, contrary to His Word; or beside it, if matters of faith, or worship. So that, to believe such doctrines, or to obey such commands, out of conscience, is to betray true liberty of conscience: and the requiring of an implicit faith, and an absolute and blind obedience, is to destroy liberty of conscience, and reason also.

III. They who, upon pretence of Christian liberty, do practise any sin, or cherish any lust, do thereby destroy the end of Christian liberty, which is, that being delivered out of the hands of our enemies, we might serve the Lord without fear, in holiness and righteousness before Him, all the days of our life.

IV. And because the powers which God hath ordained, and the liberty which Christ hath purchased, are not intended by God to destroy, but mutually to uphold and preserve one another, they who, upon pretence of Christian liberty, shall oppose any lawful power, or the lawful exercise of it, whether it be civil or ecclesiastical, resist the ordinance of God. And, for their publishing of such opinions, or maintaining of such practices, as are contrary to the light of nature, or to the known principles of Christianity (whether concerning faith, worship, or conversation), or to the power of godliness; or, such erroneous opinions or practices, as either in their own nature, or in the manner of publishing or maintaining them, are destructive to the external peace and order which Christ hath established in the Church, they may lawfully be called to account, and proceeded against, by the censures of the Church, and by the power of the civil magistrate.

Chapter XXI: '. . . . the Sabbath Day'

The strict observance of the Sabbath in Ulster is reflected in the following:

VII. As it is the law of nature, that, in general, a due proportion of time be set apart for the worship of God; so, in His Word, by a positive, moral, and perpetual commandment binding all men in all ages, He hath particularly appointed one day in seven, for a Sabbath, to be kept holy unto Him: which, from the beginning of the world to the resurrection of Christ, was the last day of the week; and, from the resurrection of Christ, was changed into the first day of the week, which, in Scripture, is called the Lord's Day, and is to be continued to the end of the world, as the Christian Sabbath.

VIII. This Sabbath is then kept holy unto the Lord, when men, after a due preparing of their hearts, and ordering of their common affairs beforehand, do not only observe an holy rest, all the day, from their own works, words, and thoughts about their worldly employments and recreations, but also are taken up, the whole time, in the public and private exercises of His worship, and in the duties of necessity and mercy.

Chapter XXIII: 'Of the Civil Magistrate'

The Confession spells out in some detail the powers of the magistrate and his relation to the state.

GOD, the supreme Lord and King of all the world, hath ordained civil magistrates, to be, under Him, over the people, for His own glory, and the public good: and, to this end, hath armed them with the power of the sword, for the defence and encouragement of them that are good, and for the punishment of evil doers.

II. It is lawful for Christians to accept and execute the office of a magistrate, when called thereunto: in the managing whereof, as they ought especially to maintain piety, justice, and peace, according to the wholesome laws of each commonwealth; so, for that end, they may lawfully, now under the new testament, wage war, upon just and necessary occasion.

III. The civil magistrate may not assume to himself the administration of the Word and sacraments, or the power of the keys of the kingdom of heaven: yet he hath authority, and it is his duty, to take order that unity and peace be preserved in the Church, that the truth of God be kept pure and entire, that all blasphemies and heresies be suppressed, all corruptions and abuses in worship and discipline prevented or reformed, and all the ordinances of God duly settled, administered, and observed. For the better effecting whereof, he hath power to call synods, to be present at them, and to provide that whatsoever is transacted in them be according to the mind of God.

IV. It is the duty of people to pray for magistrates, to honour their persons, to pay them tribute or other dues, to obey their lawful commands, and to be subject to their authority, for conscience' sake. Infidelity, or difference in religion, doth not make void the magistrates' just and legal authority, nor free the people from their due obedience to them: from which ecclesiastical persons are not exempted, much less hath the Pope any power and jurisdiction over them in their dominions, or over any of their people; and, least of all, to deprive them of their dominions, or lives, if he shall judge them to be heretics. or upon any other pretence whatsoever.

Chapter XXIV: 'Of Marriage and Divorce'

The *Confession* is as strict about 'mixed marriages' and 'divorce' as the Catholic Church.

MARRIAGE is to be between one man and one woman: neither is it lawful for any man to have more than one wife, nor for any woman to have more than one husband, at the same time.

II. Marriage was ordained for the mutual help of husband and wife, for the increase of mankind with a legitimate issue, and of the Church with an holy seed; and for preventing of uncleanness.

III. It is lawful for all sorts of people to marry, who are able with judgment to give their consent. Yet is it the duty of Christians to marry only in the Lord. And therefore such as profess the true reformed religion should not marry with infidels, papists, or other idolaters: neither should such as are godly be unequally yoked, by marrying with such as are notoriously wicked in their life, or maintain damnable heresies.

IV. Marriage ought not to be within the degrees of consanguinity or affinity forbidden by the Word. Nor can such incestuous marriages ever be made lawful by any law of man or consent of parties, so as those persons may live together as man and wife. The man may not marry any of his wife's kindred, nearer in blood than he may of his own: nor the woman of her husband's kindred, nearer in blood than of her own.

V. Adultery or fornication committed after a contract, being detected before marriage, giveth just occasion to the innocent party to dissolve that contract. In the case of adultery after marriage, it is lawful for the innocent party to sue out a divorce: and, after the divorce, to marry another, as if the offending party were dead.

VI. Although the corruption of man be such as is apt to study arguments unduly to put asunder those whom God hath joined together in marriage: yet, nothing but adultery, or such wilful desertion as can no way be remedied by the Church, or civil magistrate, is cause sufficient of dissolving the bond of marriage: wherein, a public and orderly course of proceeding is to be observed; and the persons concerned in it not left to their own wills, and discretion, in their own case.

Chapter XXV: 'Of the Church'

The *Confession* rejects the Pope as head of the Church and sees him as the representative of evil. These clauses have been set aside by the Church of Scotland, but are still maintained by the Irish Assembly.

THE catholic or universal Church, which is invisible, consists of the whole number of the elect, that have been, are, or shall be gathered into one, under Christ the Head thereof; and is the spouse, the body, the fulness of Him that filleth all in all.

II. The visible Church, which is also catholic or universal under the Gospel (not confined to one nation, as before under the law), consists of all those throughout the world that profess the true religion; and of their children: and is the kingdom of the Lord Jesus Christ, the house and family of God, out of which there is no ordinary possibility of salvation.

III. Unto this catholic visible Church Christ hath given the ministry, oracles, and ordinances of God, for the gathering and perfecting of the saints, in this life, to the end of the world: and doth, by His own presence and Spirit, according to His promise, make them effectual thereunto.

IV. This catholic Church hath been sometimes more, sometimes less visible. And particular Churches, which are members thereof, are more or less pure, according as the doctrine of the Gospel is taught and embraced, ordinances administered, and public worship performed more or less purely in them.

V. The purest Churches under heaven are subject both to mixture and error; and some have so degenerated, as to become no Churches of Christ, but synagogues of Satan. Nevertheless, there shall be always a Church on earth, to worship God according to His will.

VI. There is no other head of the Church but the Lord Jesus Christ. Nor can the Pope of Rome, in any sense, be head thereof: but is that Antichrist, that man of sin, and son of perdition, that exalteth himself, in the Church, against Christ and all that is called God.

INDEX

Act of Supremacy, 42, 130
Act of Uniformity, 42, 131
Act of Union, 25, 48, 135
African National Congress (A.N.C.), 111, 113, 114–16
Afrikaners, 103, 106ff
Alliance Party, 10, 81, 124
Anglo-Irish ascendancy, 42, 48, 79
Anglo-Irish Accord (Hillsborough), 63, 90, 100ff, 113, 119, 125–6
Anglican Church, *see* Church of Ireland
Anne, Queen, 45
Antrim, Co., 20
Apprentice Boys, ix, 23, 24, 29
Armagh, 11, 20, 41,
Asquith, Herbert, 31, 33, 35, 36
Aughrim, 28

Baker, Major Henry, 23
Barr, Glenn, 92
Barritt and Carter, 67
Bastille, fall of the, 47
battles: *see* Boyne, Somme
Beckett J.C., 42, 47, 59
Belfast: 1, 2, 3, 5, 10, 11, 21, 24, 31, 32, 44, 69; City Hall, 26, 69; Shipyards, 75; *see also* Falls Road, Shankill Road
Belfast Telegraph, 44
Bell, Bowyer, 97
Biko, Steve, 111
Bill of Rights, 116
Boesak, Allan, 109
Boland, Kevin, 86
Border, North-South, question, 61, 67–9, 71
Botha P.W., 111–14
Boundary Commission, 62, 116
Boyne, battle of the, 1, 2, 3, 24, 28, 45, 47, 58, 69, 82, 107
Broederbond, Afrikaner, 82, 110
Brookeborough, Lord, 61, 67–9
'B Specials', ix, 37, 62, 79
Buthelezi, Chief Gatsha 116

Callaghan, James, 78–9

Calvin, Calvinism, 52, 56, 57
Cameron Commission, 66, 73, 39
Campaign for Social Justice, 75
Carson, Edward, 31–2, 35–7, 74
Carson, Rt Revd John T., 74
Catholic Association, 49; special position in Irish constitution, 65
Catholic Church, Catholicism, 10–13, 14–17, 42, 45f, 48, 53–9, 62, 64ff, 94, 120, 125
Catholic Emancipation, 49, 51, 136
Catholic Relief Act, 48, 133
Catholic people, population, 1, 3, 4, 10, 14–18, 46–59, 98–101; discrimination against, 62–3, 74–6, 107
Cavan, Co., 20
Celtic football team, 5
Charles II, King, 22
Chichester-Clark, Major James, 79
Church of Ireland (Anglican), 4, 10, 23, 25, 42, 43, 44, 56–7
Church of Scotland, 122
Churchill, Lord Randolph, 3; opposition to Home Rule, 26
Churchill, Winston, 3–4, 26, 37, 55
Civil Rights Movement, ix, 65–6, 70, 71, 73, 74, 75, 77, 81, 106
Civil War, 36–7
Clark, George, 68
Coleraine, 20
Columba, St, 41
Columbanus, St, 41
Common Prayer, Book of, 42
Commonwealth 'Eminent Persons Group', 114
Conservative Party (British), 33, 54
Constitution of Republic of Ireland, 119
Constitutional Convention (1974), 89, 90
Conway, Cardinal W. (Archbishop of Armagh), 65, 69, 73, 121
Cooke, Henry, 25, 49ff
Corrigan, Mairead, 93
Cosgrave, Liam, 86
Council of Ireland, 63, 86

148

Covenant, 29, 34–5, 54–5
Curtis, E., 21, 41, 54
Craig, James (Lord Craigavon), 31–3, 35, 36, 61, 62, 63, 85, 87, 88, 121
Craig, William, 78, 87, 88, 90–1, 107; *see also* Vanguard
Criminal Justice Act, 89
Cromwell, Oliver, 21–2, 45

Daly, Edward (R.C. Bishop of Derry), 94
Darlington, 96
Democratic Unionist Party, ix, 91, 96, 101–2
Derry: 7, 8, 23, 70, 71, 74; siege of, 17, 23–4, 28, 45, 58, 63, 87; 'Bloody Sunday', 80
detention without trial, 110
De Valera, Eamon, 36, 37, 63, 71
Devlin, Bernadette, 66, 76
Devlin, Joseph, 55
discrimination, *see* Catholics
Doherty, Peter, 5
Donegal, Co., 20, 94
Down, Co., 20
Doyle, James (Bishop of Kildare), 66
Drogheda, 22
Drummond, Thomas, 28
Dublin, 8, 31, 32, 34, 97; parliament, 33, 42, 62, 97, 102
Dutch Reformed Church, 106, 107, 108–10, 112

Easter Rising (1916), 36, 64, 68
Ecumenical Movement, 58
education, religious separation in, 15, 32, 65–7, 69, 70–1, 75, 97, 120–2
Elizabeth II, Queen, 74
Enniskillen, Earl of, 29
Evangelical Union, 7
Evangelicalism, 7, 8–9, 13–14, 42, 52, 55–6, 64,

Falls Road, 29, 56, 72, 108
Farrell, Michael, 76
Faulkner, Brian, 29–30, 76–7, 79–80, 82, 86, 88, 111
Feakle, meeting at, 94–5

'Fenian', 25–6, 33, 93
Fermanagh, Co., 20
Fianna Fail party, 37
Fitt, Gerry, 80, 86, 118
Fitzgerald, Dr Garret, 78, 100
Fraser, Hugh, 126
Free Presbyterian Church of Ulster, 13, 72
Fulton, Rt Revd Austin, 73
Future of Northern Ireland: Paper for Discussion 140ff.

Gaels, The 40
Gallaher and Worrall, 95
General Assembly, 16, 51, 73
Genesis stories, 7
George V, King, 34, 35
Gladstone, W.E., 26, 27, 31
Gough, General Sir Hubert, 35
Gow, Ian, 102
Graham, Sir Clarence, 68
Great Trek, 107
Group Areas Act, 107
Gun-running, 32

'H' Block, 96
Hanna, Revd Hugh, 87–8
Hanna, Robert, 67–8
Haughey, Charles, 102
Heath, Edward, 80, 85, 86,
Henry VIII, King, 9, 41–2, 57, 108
Higgins, Kevin, 37
Hillsborough, *see* Anglo-Irish Accord
Holland, Jack, 92
Home Rule Bills: first (1886), 26–7, 136; second (1892), 30–1; third (under Asquith), 30, 31, 32–6, 55, 87; and religion, 53–5
Hull, Roger H., 98
Hume, John, 118

Irish Republican Army (I.R.A.), ix, 8, 25, 36–7, 62, 64, 71, 74, 92, 97, 121, 126; statements of leaders, 140; *see also* Provisional I.R.A.
Irish Republican Brotherhood, 33, 36, 64

James I, King, 20
James II, King, 22-3, 28, 45, 58, 87
Jenkins, David (Bishop of Durham), 58, 126
John XXIII, Pope, 69
John Paul II, Pope, 45, 95

Kee, Robert, 23
Keswick Convention, 13, 52,
Kennedy, John F., 70
King, Tom, 103

Law, Andrew Bonar, 33
League of Prayer and Reconciliation, 94
Lemass, Sean (President of Irish Republic), visit to Belfast, 69, 70, 74, 79
linen industry, 24, 33
Lloyd George, David, 36
Lockwood, Sir John, 70
Londonderry, *see* Derry
Londonderry, Lord, 121
Longford, Lord, 78, 93
Louis XIV, King of France, 22, 24
loyalty to British Crown, Loyalism: 31, 32, 37, 51, 87-9; conditional, 88
Lundy, Colonel Robert, 23, 24
Luther, Martin, 57
Lyons, F.S.L., 44

Macaulay, Lord, 82
McCann, Eamon, 76
MacEoin, Gary, 66
Macmillan, Harold, 70
MacStiofain, Sean, 98
Magee College, Derry, 7, 10, 66
Magee, John, 62
Maginess, Brian, 67-8
Malan, D.F., 110
Mandela, Nelson, 115
Mary I, Queen, 57
Mary II, Queen, 22
Mason, Roy, 96
Matthew, Dr Robert, 70
Meyer, P.J., 110
Mitchell, John, 26
'mixed marriages', 15, 54, 64, 66-7
Mixed Marriages Act, 109

Mountbatten, Lord, 89
Montgomery, Henry, 50-1

Napier, Oliver, ix, 124
Naudé, Beyers, 110
Ne Temere decree, 54, 67, 111
New University of Ulster, 66, 70
Newe, Dr Gerald, 80
Newry, 14, 71
Northern Ireland Assembly 103

'Oak-Boys', 47
O'Brien, Smith, 26
O'Connell, Daniel, 25, 26, 29, 49, 54
O'Connell, David, 92
O'Dwyer, Edward (Bishop of Limerick), 64
O'Neill, Phelim, 29
O'Neill, Terence, 17, 68-73, 76-81, 114
O'Neills, the, 19ff.
O'Shea, Katherine, 27, 54
opinion polls and surveys 87, 99, 120
Orange Boys, 27
Orange Order, Orangeism: 2ff, 10, 12, 27-30, 48, 49, 55, 81-2, 94, 96, 110, 121
Orange rules, 134

Paisley, Ian, 13ff, 72-3, 74, 76, 85, 86, 87-90, 95, 122; *see also* Democratic Unionist Party, Free Presbyterian Church
Parnell, Charles Stewart, 26, 27, 53, 54
Partition, 59, 61
Patrick, Saint, 40, 41, 59n.
Peace Movement, 92-3
Pearse, Patrick, 26
Peep O'Day Boys, 27
Peoples' Democracy, ix, 71, 76
Pitt, William, the Younger, 48, 49
Plantation, 20ff, 131
Pope, the: 42, 45-6, 123; Protestant condemnation of, 9, 51, 123
Portstewart, 13, 52, 68
power-sharing, 86
Presbyterian Church: of Ireland, vii, 9, 13, 16; and role of laity, 43; and

Index

preaching, 44; General Assembly, 16, 43, 58, 73, 77, 95; Synod 43, 48, 52, 55; — of Scotland, 43–4, 122–3
Presbyterianism, 4, 42f, 46f
Princeton Seminary, 9
Proportional Representation, 62, 85
Protestant, Protestantism: social attitudes, 3–4, 5, 15–17; trait of independence, 31, 87; anti-Catholic feeling, 45–9 *passim*, 63, 69, 74, 77, 82, 98–9; land ownership after Plantation, 20–3; and events of 1689–90, 23–4, 29, 58; possible changes in hardline attitude, 89ff., 123–4; *see also* Anglo-Irish Accord, Covenant, education, Home Rule, Orange Order
Protestant demands, 133
Protestant Telegraph, 72
Provisional I.R.A., 92, 94, 95
Provisional Sinn Fein, 95
Pym, Francis, 96

Queen's University, Belfast, 17, 65, 75

Rangers football team, 5
Redmond, John, 33, 36, 55, 64
Rees, Merlyn, 83, 95f
Reformation, 9, 57, 125
Regium Donum, 46, 49
Richardson, George, 35
Robinson, John (Bishop), 58
Robinson, Peter, 103
Rose, Richard, 88, 123
Royal Ulster Constabulary, 72, 79, 101

Sabbath, observance of the, 44
Sash, The (song), 2–3
Scarman Tribunal, 139
Shankill Road (Belfast), 10, 11, 29, 56, 93, 108, 127
Sinn Fein, 36, 37, 72
Smuts, J.C., 112
Smyth, Revd Martin, 13, 88, 89
Social Democratic and Labour Party (S.D.L.P.), 80, 89, 91, 96, 118–19
Somme, battle of the, 29, 63, 74

Soweto, 114
Special Powers Act, 62, 111
Spencer, Sir Wilfred, 63
Statutes of Kilkenny, 108
'Steel-Boys', 47
Stephens, James, 26
Stewart, A.T.Q., 40, 56
Stewart, Dr Kenneth, 123
Stormont (Ulster parliament), 36, 53, 61ff, 72, 80, 81, 85, 88, 121, 127
Stronge, Sir Norman, 12
Subscription (to *Westminster Confession*) controversy, 50–2
Sunningdale Conference (1973), 86, 96

Terre Blanche, Eugene, 112
Thatcher, Mrs, 100, 102ff, 112
Thirty-Nine Articles, 42
Tone, Wolfe, 47
Treaty between Great Britain and Ireland, 138
Treurnicht, Andries, 112
Trinity College, Dublin, 1, 8, 42, 46, 48
Triracial Party, 111
Tyrconnel, Earl of, 20

Ulster Constitution Defence Committee, 72
Ulster Defence Association, 91–2, 94
Ulster Defence Regiment, 79
Ulster Special Constabulary, 37
Ulster Unionist Council, 18, 30
Ulster Unionist Party, 17, 68
Ulster Volunteer Force, 32, 63, 74, 78, 79, 94
Ulster Workers' Council, 86, 87
Union, Act of, *see* Act of Union
Unionist Party of Northern Ireland, 49, 88
United Irishmen, 25, 47, 48, 51, 78, 134
United States of America, 91, 92, 98, 99
United Ulster Unionist Council, 87, 91
University of Ulster, 66, 70

Vanguard Unionist Party, 90, 96
Verwoerd, Dr Hendrik, 110

Walker, Revd George, 23

Wallace, Martin, 67
Washington, George, on Scotch-Irish, 24
Weber, Max, 56
Wesley, John, 128
West, Harry, 79, 87, 88, 91,
Westminster Confession of Faith (1643), 9, 42, 50–1, 107, 122, 143–8
'White-Boys', 47
Whitelaw, William, 83, 96
Wilde, Oscar, 31

William III, King (Prince of Orange, 'King Billy'), 1, 2, 22–4, 27, 28, 29, 45, 46
Williams, Betty, 93
Wilson, Harold, 70, 78, 86, 87, 97
working class: 26; appeal of Paisleyism to, 13–14
World Council of Churches, 55, 58, 81, 95, 109

Zulus, 107